Howard Zehr's dedication to cannot be overstated. He has been the issue. His teaching, mentorshi marked my work and my journey a ca's most brutal civil wars.

I was privileged to spend four days with Howard at the Pennsylvania State Penitentiary as part of our course work in 2007. I saw his compassion and respect for incarcerated men and their opinion on justice issues.

Our world, our journey as peacebuilders, and the global community are a better place because of this great man's service to humanity!

—*Leymah R. Gbowee, Nobel Peace Prize winner, Liberia*

Inside a 30-foot-high concrete wall is where I met Howard. That was in 2009. I was fighting a death by incarceration sentence and had just cofounded an RJ project based largely on his writings.

Through the years we would become colleagues, friends, and brothers. And while his impact on the movement is clear, it's his humility and quiet wisdom that continue to infect me most.

That's as true today as in that prison classroom thirteen years ago.

—*Felix Rosado, recently released from prison, author of*
Let's Circle Up: Doing Restorative Justice Education Together

Howard has long resisted talking about himself, despite proddings from those of us who cherish what he personally brings to the field of Restorative Justice: his loving, open, principled heart, his vast experiences with amazing people, and his dance between deep reverence for the human condition and playful irreverence for its foibles.

I'm thrilled that he's finally written something that shares his very human journey to his profound contributions to our field.

—*sujatha baliga, attorney and Restorative Justice practitioner (winner of the MacArthur Fellowship)*

This memoir of Howard's life lifts the curtain on a humble, faithful prophet who has given the next generation one of the greatest gifts: *A justice that heals and transforms!*

—*Carl Stauffer, Ph.D., United States Institute of Peace, Washington, D.C.*

Howard has always been both extraordinary—and extraordinarily humble.

He has taught so many of us—directly or indirectly—but so much of what distinguishes his brilliance is that he has also learned from so many people in the movement for so long. This continuous learning, rooted in his unending regard for the value of other people, is as much the spirit of Restorative Justice as all the other work he has developed and led through his lastingly impactful career.

—*Danielle Sered, Common Justice, Founder/Director*

Howard's classes were legendary; his students were always profoundly impacted by his philosophy.

As a teacher, he epitomized the Indian concept of "guru" and remains my most loved and respected mentor. Thank you, Howard.

—*Sudipta Bhattacharjee, editor and media science professor, India*

In a prison cell, I first read *The Little Book of Restorative Justice* by Howard Zehr.

At the time, I was unaware of the impact of that moment.

In class, at EMU a decade later, I listened as Dr. Zehr expounded the history and theory of RJ. In a series of meetings and engagements that semester, he became a mentor and a friend.

In 2017, Howard was the commencement speaker when I became the first graduate with a Master's Degree in Restorative Justice. Like others who follow in Howard's footsteps, mine is a story of transformation and the healing power of Restorative Justice.

—*Gregory Winship, Restorative Justice strategist/Justice Involved, Center for Conflict Resolution, Kansas City, MO*

TRIBUTES AND ENDORSEMENTS

I can't think of anyone other than Howard who gets the nuances of Restorative Justice and distills them so simply and clearly.

—*David Karp, director, Center for Restorative Justice, University of San Diego*

The book is equally instructive and enjoyable for both the RJ novice and the seasoned practitioner. Howard's reflections on his decades of experience remind us of the humanity in our work and guide how we may maintain hope when facing the challenges of integrating love into our most powerful judicial institutions.

—*Brenda Waugh, lawyer, mediator, Restorative Justice facilitator*

Howard is a steady pioneer with a sustained vision, a unique combination of opposites that characterizes true leaders in all social movements.

These are the gifts that he has brought to the Restorative movement—both the vision and the spirit to sustain it.

To our generation he has taught that the struggle for justice is long and hard, and thinking that it can be won within a lifetime is thinking small. He has also taught us that for our vision to be credible we have to walk the talk, and for it to be shared, we have to walk it with others.

—*Dr. Brunilda Pali, senior researcher, University of Leuven, Belgium*

I knew that I was "stepping into the unknown" by adapting Restorative Justice principles in federal death penalty cases.

One of Howard's incredible gifts is that he encourages the path unseen in both his students and in society, with a wink to what is possible. The principles that Howard honed remain a beacon for those working in the field.

His contributions to creating a more healing legal system are profound and enduring.

—*Tammy Krause, Ph.D., co-chair of National Council for Defense-Victim Outreach*

TRIBUTES AND ENDORSEMENTS

This absorbing and creative book is a treasure-trove of personal reminiscences, historical tidbits, and seasoned insights into the philosophy and practice of Restorative Justice by its most influential pioneer.

It also bears testimony to a mind and a life lived so graciously and generously in service of others.

—Chris Marshall, emeritus professor, Te Ngāpara Centre for Restorative Practice, Victoria University of Wellington, New Zealand

We are grateful to Howard for the way he helped us see and understand how to build our practice on a bedrock of values and principles.

—Catherine Bargen, co-founder of Just Outcomes

This book is such an authentic window into who Howard is beyond the reflectors and titles:

- a loving husband of Ruby;
- a passionate traveler and photographer with a great sense of humor;
- someone bright, with a sharp curiosity for history, people, life, and knowledge;
- with a humble and generous heart.

—Katia Ornelas, Restorative Justice practitioner, Mexico City, Mexico

This personalized account of the creation and development of the Restorative Justice movement offers fresh and illuminating insights.

This is indispensable for anybody interested in the history of contemporary Restorative Justice, or indeed for anybody curious about crime and how we might handle it better.

—Gerry Johnstone, Professor of Law, University of Hull, UK and author of Restorative Justice: Ideas, Values, Debates

CONTINUED ON PAGE 81—

Restorative Justice –

Insights and Stories from My Journey

Howard Zehr

WALNUT
STREET
BOOKS

LANCASTER,
PENNSYLVANIA

walnutstreetbooks.com

Cover and page design by Cliff Snyder and Mike Bond

Contents

Who is Howard Zehr?

Howard Zehr is widely recognized as one of the founders and early pioneers of the Restorative Justice field. In his role as director of a national criminal justice resource office, then as professor of Restorative Justice in an international graduate program, he has assisted and mentored many individuals and organizations. He has lectured and consulted in numerous countries.

His many publications include *Changing Lenses*, the book that helped to define the field initially, and the best-selling *Little Book of Restorative Justice*. Many of these books have been translated and published in other languages.

He has also been a professional photographer and has published a number of books based on photography that are cited later.

"No person has done more to inspire the restorative imagination of citizens of this planet than Howard Zehr."

– John Braithwaite, Distinguished Professor, Australian National University

More information is included in About the Author on page 216.

Beginning the Journey

B efore there was "Restorative Justice" there was VORP. The Victim Offender Reconciliation Program or Project (VORP) began in Elmira, Ontario, in 1974 and in Elkhart, Indiana, soon thereafter. The Elkhart effort, developed by chief juvenile probation officer Steve Miller and several other probation officers, was housed in the juvenile probation department. By the time I arrived on the scene in 1978 and assumed leadership of the effort, the program had handled a number of cases but was somewhat stalled.

The idea behind victim offender "reconciliation" (we later dropped the term because it was misleading) was to allow those crime victims who were willing to do so to meet with the person who had harmed them, facilitated by a trained facilitator. This provided an opportunity for those who were harmed to put a face to the person who had done it, to express their feelings and tell their stories, to get answers to their many questions, and to receive some measure of restitution for the harm done.

For those who had caused harm, it provided an opportunity to understand the impact of their actions on people and to take responsibility for it. In the best of scenarios, it allowed for some understanding and empathy for all. By using trained community facilitators, the approach allowed for some involvement and representation of the larger community.

Howard being interviewed on the subway by a reporter for a national newspaper while on a speaking tour in Japan, 2006.

I was a reluctant participant initially. My justice involvements had been on the side of defendants and prisoners. I knew nothing about the experiences of victims, and I was very reluctant to collaborate with "the system." But it didn't take long, seeing what happened when "victims" and "offenders" met, for my understandings to change.

Early on our program had restricted itself to juvenile cases such as burglary, vandalism, and theft. Because of the success of these efforts, probation officer Lonnie Buerge—my key contact in the department—suggested that it was time to tackle a serious adult case. He proposed the case of Harry Fred Palmer, convicted in 1978 of at least a dozen serious house burglaries in the county.

Among those Fred victimized was Randy Yohn and his family. Unknown to Fred until he broke into the house, Randy was Chief Deputy Sheriff of Elkhart County. Randy and his wife were open to meeting with Fred in their home—the place he had violated—in part so that he would be confronted with the meaning of what he had done and so that any differences about damages could be resolved. That meeting, which Lonnie and I facilitated, went well. Fred was very emotional when confronted with the impact of what he had done, and the family found the meeting helpful.

Based on the success of that case, we decided to tackle another of Fred's cases. While Randy and Tonya Brown were on their honeymoon, Fred had backed a truck up to their house and cleaned out their belongings.

"If I had been there, I could easily have shot him," Randy Brown said. In fact, we later learned that in a previous holdup, Randy had wrestled the gun away from his assailant and shot him. Randy was eager for a confrontation, but it turned out quite differently than he expected. As he talked with Fred, Randy began to understand and identify with him. "Fred and I have a lot in common," he suggested. For restitution, Randy and Tonya asked Fred to come to their place on weekends and chop wood. "If it had been me," Randy said, "I'm not sure whether I would have chosen prison, rather than face the people I had harmed."

Given such outcomes, and the fact that Fred had been law-abiding until scarred by his military service in Vietnam, Judge William Bontrager decided that, instead of the mandatory sentence of 10-20 years, Fred would be better off if he experienced enough prison to understand the seriousness of what he had done, but not so much that he would be damaged by it. Fred was sentenced to 205 days. Then he was to return to the community and make restitution for his harms.

Unfortunately, the story does not end there. The prosecutor appealed this "extremely peculiar sentence," and it was overturned by the Indiana Supreme Court. Three years after leaving prison, Fred was ordered to return and serve the remainder of a mandatory 10-20 year indeterminate sentence.

During those three years of freedom, Fred had been making restitution and had become friends with Randy Yohn. The case also made national news and eventually was documented in a national TV documentary hosted by tough-guy actor George Kennedy, entitled "Going Straight." In the film, Randy is seen driving in his sheriff's car to the prison to visit Fred. He comments that while Fred was out of prison, he had told Fred that he was going on vacation. Then he thought, "I just told my burglar that I was going to be gone! But I believe Fred would have watched my house better than I could."

Fred and his family had become part of our church community at Southside Mennonite Fellowship. The group helped to mount a campaign to obtain a commutation from the governor, which was eventually granted. Randy Yohn went on to become Sheriff of Elkhart County and to serve on the board of our program. In his retirement, he served briefly as director. Judge Bontrager was fined for contempt of court. He eventually left the bench, due in part to his opposition to mandatory sentences, and moved to Eastern Europe to teach law and Restorative Justice.

Although this was the most remarkable of those early cases, experiences like this forced me to rethink what I thought I knew about justice, to "change my lens." As I tried to articulate what we were learning, I realized that all this had much bigger implications than simply victim-offender encounters. I began to pull together a variety of streams of thought and experiences into an overall concept or philosophy. Needing a name that would resonate with people, I discovered the term "restorative justice" mentioned briefly in an article by Albert Eglash and adopted it as a name for the concept.

I had forgotten where I got the term until South African researcher Anne Skelton visited my office and found it underlined in an Eglash essay in a book on my shelf. She traced the term back to a German theologian in the 1950s. But Danish researcher Christian B. N. Gade, in the book *Nordic Mediation Research*, since then found the term used in various contexts as far back as 1834.

One of the current controversies in the Restorative Justice field is the extent to which it has been based on, and has even appropriated, indigenous justice approaches. I am sorry to say that at the time I was developing my thinking, I was almost totally ignorant of those traditions. Rather, I developed my thinking from my own western "indigenous" traditions—historical, religious, experiential—and only later learned the many important points of resonance with many indigenous traditions. More about that later.

About this book

I have explained and developed my understanding of Restorative Justice in many publications and lectures over the years. Best known of these are the books *Changing Lenses* and *The Little Book of Restorative Justice*. This book includes essays and talks related to Restorative Justice that are not as readily available. Included also are some reflections on photography, a medium that has been

For many years I worked part-time as a photographer. On one of my photojournalism assignments for Mennonite Central Committee (MCC), I traveled with an MCC veterinarian couple in northern Kenya who maintained a model camel herd. As befitting MCC and Restorative Justice values, they were very relational camels!

as important to me in the search for justice as has been the written word.

To put together the selection for this book, I gave editor Phyllis Pellman Good a variety of essays and talks and let her decide which seemed to make the most coherent and useful collection. We then adapted them in minor ways. For example, we have worked to reduce repetition, but to maintain the integrity of each piece, some repetition remains. For the sake of simplicity, references are not included but may be found in the original publications.

Phyllis and her husband Merle—my long-term publishers—also urged me to add some stories and photos from my life and work. Not being very interested in autobiographical writing, I was very reluctant but eventually agreed to include some, including a chapter about my long involvement in amateur radio.

In the following chapters, I have provided brief introductions to the essays or lectures to provide contexts. I have also added a few sidebars with explanations or stories and concluded most chapters with a section of reflections and/or stories and sometimes photos. The introductions and concluding reflections, which are not part of the original essay or talk, are indicated by a change of fonts.

Some of this will feel like the musings and reminiscences of an old man, for good reason. This book appears at a stage in my life when I am consciously seeking to be a "has been." After almost half a century in the field, it is time to truly retire and make space for others. For this reason, I have had mixed feelings about further publishing. It is because of Phyllis and Merle's vision, encouragement, and support that this book has been published by their Walnut Street Books.

When I got involved in VORP, one of my first publications was a how-to manual entitled "The VORP Book" made up of various chapters. Chapter II was an overview of the process. I illustrated the last steps and— unfortunately, as I look back—ended rather naïvely:
That's really all there is to it.
A dash of this,
A form for that
Follow the recipe,
Flavor to taste,
And that's all it takes to cook up a VORP!

PART 1

What Exactly Is Restorative Justice?

CHAPTER ONE

Restorative Justice– The Promise, the Challenge

A conversation with
Katia Cecilia Ornelas-Nuñez

*R*estorative Justice has garnered much interest in Mexico. In 2014, the Alternative Dispute Resolution Center of the Judicial Power of the State of Tamaulipas invited me to present to a conference. For that I was interviewed by Katia Cecilia Ornelas-Nuñez , a Mexican lawyer with experience working to transform Mexico's criminal justice system and the defense of human and women's rights. As an M.A. graduate of our program, the Center for Justice and Peacebuilding (CJP) at Eastern Mennonite University, and as a friend, Katia was an ideal conversation partner.

This interview is focused primarily on applications of Restorative Justice within, or in collaboration with, the criminal (as opposed to civil) legal system. But as will be clear throughout this collection, Restorative Justice today *has much wider areas of application, some of which are intentionally independent of formal institutions such as the legal system.*

Howard and Katia (left) on the conference platform.

Katia Ornelas (KO): What is Restorative Justice (RJ)? How is it different from the punitive criminal justice system?

Howard Zehr (HZ): Restorative Justice first started as an effort to deal with crime in a better way. Now it is also being used in schools and lots of other areas, but our first concern was with the criminal justice system. A case in 1974 in Canada is considered to have started all of this. And then, at about the same time in northern Indiana, some probation officers had a similar idea and began working with it. I came on the scene during the late 1970s. I was asked to pick up this idea that had very little shape or definition.

I immediately began to write handbooks, sketching out how I imagined it could be done. Already in the late '70s and early '80s, people were coming from Germany, England, and other countries, and then they'd go home and start implementing some of what they had observed.

In the 1980s, both the U.K. and Germany instituted various forms of victim-offender conferencing that eventually evolved into other innovative applications of Restorative Justice.

So the idea, which eventually became Restorative Justice, started to take off. At that time, it didn't have a theory or a name. We were just trying to solve a problem. We didn't have a theoretical framework for the concept.

KO: What were you trying to solve?

HZ: We had three big concerns. First, we knew that as a society we were punishing a lot of people. But we weren't holding them accountable in any meaningful way, or in a way that helped them really understand and take responsibility for what they did.

Second, we were concerned about victims. Not only were they being left out, but they were often being retraumatized in the "justice" process.

And third, we were concerned about the community being left out. We really believed that a community is strengthened when it becomes engaged in these issues. When we turn everything over to the criminal justice system, we disempower the community.

So initially, we didn't have an overall philosophy in mind. Instead, we began by bringing victims and offenders together—those who were willing to meet—to talk about what happened. Victims could express their anger, tell their story, and get some answers to their questions. Offenders could hear the victims' experiences.

RJ is often thought of as a model that allows victims and offenders to come together. That is *part* of RJ's work—"victim-offender conferencing," family group conferences and circles, and other similar groups. Early on, RJ was primarily an effort to bring those who had been harmed and those who had caused the harm together in a facilitated process. These were people who had been harmed, and people who had caused harm. As we've had more experience, we've realized that it's much more than that. A whole continuum of approaches implements Restorative Justice principles. Some are more restorative than others. For example, a prisoner reentry program might use a family conference to help plan reintegration. It might reach out to the prisoner's victims to see what they need. But it may not necessarily bring victim and offender together.

KO: If RJ is not a program or particular model, what is its essence?

HZ: What really matters are its principles or its concept of justice. And this is where it differs sharply from the criminal justice system.

The criminal justice system tends to ask three questions:

- What laws were broken?
- Who did it?
- What do they deserve?

Everything focuses around making sure offenders get what they deserve. That is usually punishment.

There is nothing for the victim because the victim isn't really a part of the criminal justice system. The crime is considered to be against the government, against the state.

Restorative Justice changes the questions. It asks:

- Who's been hurt in the situation?
- What are their needs?
- Whose obligations are they?

Restorative Justice focuses on needs and obligations and not so much on what the offender deserves. The victim is just as important as the offender in this process. RJ turns the situation so that the victim's needs are addressed and the offender's obligations are discussed and worked with. The whole concept is based on the reality that we humans are rooted in relationships, and that relationships matter.

In its simplest form, RJ is based on three basic principles. The first is that harm has been done, and harm creates needs. What really matter are the harms. The first principle of RJ is that we need to address those harms and needs.

Second is the principle of obligations. The person who caused the harm has an obligation. And other people may have obligations as well. The second principle has to do with addressing the obligations.

Third is the principle of engagement or involvement. Those people who were impacted, or somehow have a stake in what's happened, ought to be part of the resolution.

RJ is a relational, needs-based concept of justice rather than a legalistic, offender-oriented, deserts-based concept of justice.

Today there are lots of programs, but what is ultimately important is the framework, the approach to justice. For instance, my lawyer friends who practice criminal law increasingly ask themselves with each case, who has been hurt, what are their needs, whose obligations are they, and how can we engage all the appropriate people in this process? Even without Restorative Justice programs as such, the concept is being used in a variety of creative ways. Sometimes it means that victims and offender meet; sometimes they don't.

It is also essential to combine the principles with values. Many values are part of the Restorative Justice field, but I focus on three in particular, three that start with "r" in English: respect, responsibility, and relationship. RJ demonstrates those values, and restorative approaches must be grounded in those values. If we don't treat people respectfully, we aren't practicing Restorative Justice.

KO: What are some of RJ's challenges? For example, some express concern about the softness of RJ. Is RJ soft compared to the punitive justice system?

HZ: I think many people have a misconception about what RJ is. Police officers all over the world ask, "Are you going to hold hands and sing 'Kumbaya'?" Somehow there's the belief that RJ gets offenders off the hook. Actually, it puts offenders *on* the hook more than punishment does.

RJ is very difficult to do. Facing the person you have harmed is not easy. You will experience consequences for the wrongdoing you have done. Offenders who have been in jail often say it's a lot easier to go to prison than to face their victims. We've seen gang members who were scheduled to meet with their victims start shaking as the time approaches, so that the meeting had to be delayed until they could pull themselves together. Restorative Justice does not mean there will be no consequences.

Although it may involve a face-to-face meeting, RJ is different than mediation. In mediation the parties are on a level playing field morally. In a Restorative Justice case, however, somebody has done something wrong, and a discussion of that wrong is part of the process. Restorative Justice requires naming the wrongdoing, which is an essential part of any justice process.

Agreements about the consequences are also part of the discussion. Those agreements have to be fulfilled. In some cases, these agreements will be combined with other consequences, including jail or prison time. It is a complete misunderstanding, even naïve, to think that RJ is an easy process.

KO: Does RJ insist that victims forgive their offenders? A lot of women's advocates argue against and are afraid of RJ processes because of the forgiveness component, which could put the victim in a place that could be vulnerable and retraumatizing.

HZ: That is a problematic misconception. RJ is absolutely not about forgiveness. It is about holding offenders accountable. It is about meeting victims' needs. If victims choose some degree of forgiveness, that is up to them. But reputable RJ programs do not push for forgiveness.

RJ is about meeting needs, holding offenders accountable, and engaging the people involved in the process. All of this has to be done safely. What has happened is that some people have chosen to forgive. The media love those stories and highlight them, and then the perception is that RJ and forgiveness automatically go together. Just because some people decide to forgive, doesn't mean that those two things must both happen.

We do know that many times when a victim and an offender have been carefully prepared, and then meet with the assistance of trained facilitators, tensions may reduce during the meeting, and the victim and offender may develop a better understanding of each other. We know that from research. We also know that victims are usually less traumatized when they go through this process.

The use of Restorative Justice in cases of domestic violence has been very controversial, for good reason. In these situations, Restorative Justice processes that involve direct victim and offender contact must be used very cautiously. A number of communities have developed carefully designed processes for domestic violence cases, with built-in safe-guards.

Regardless of whether direct victim-offender encounters are appropriate, the framework remains the focus on needs, harms, obligations, and engagement.

KO: Can you say more about victims being less trauma-tized because of these processes?

HZ: A major study in England a number of years ago looked at research from all over the world. It concluded that there is so much compelling evidence of reduced trauma and post-traumatic stress disorder by victims who go through RJ processes that, if applied nationally, could lower the cost of healthcare.

KO: What else could prevent victims from engaging in these processes?

HZ: Unfortunately, many programs do not involve victims and victims' advocates in their planning. I firmly believe that both victims and their advocates must be involved in every stage of developing the program and plan, because only they have the sensitivity to know if something essential is missing, if something insensitive is being done or not done, if the language is insensitive, and so on.

Often people start programs, and then they go to victims' advocates and say, "Why don't you join us?" It is a mistake not to include victims' advocates right from the beginning. The criminal justice system often does not involve victims' advocates either.

Another caution is that often Restorative Justice advocates come from backgrounds of working with offenders and don't have sufficient knowledge of, and sensitivity to, *victims'* interests and concerns. I've had offenders' organizations contact me and say, "Look at our website. Our group adopted RJ now." I look at their website, and there are 32 things you can do to help offenders and not a single thing for victims.

KO: How does a society, a country, put a Restorative Justice approach into effect in their criminal justice system—and have it work?

HZ: From my experience and my own perspective, I believe that a truly restorative approach must involve collaboration between the criminal justice system and the community.

Today there is a movement within the legal profession in the U.S. calling for better partnership between justice professionals and communities. The advocates of this collaboration say that we need each other. We need professional expertise as well, but we also need the insights and involvement of the community.

For example, Restorative Justice approaches such as circle processes have been found to empower communities to work with their issues. Kay Pranis, one of the leading advocates and trainers of circle processes in the United States, believes that circles and other restorative processes can help to "reweave" the fabric of community.

One big city drug prosecutor did a drug bust in the city, and then did a circle with drug dealers and the community they were impacting. The drug dealers heard directly how they were affecting the community. That seemed a very creative approach to a complex problem.

Ideally RJ isn't just about meeting the needs of the victims. It's also about meeting the needs of the offenders. A lot of young people who get into the drug trade do it because they don't have any other economic options, or because their families are dysfunctional. The New Zealand model uses restorative conferences, which they call Family Group Conferences. In them, they not only talk with the victims about what they need, but they also talk with offenders about what is happening in their lives, and what needs to be done to find creative ways for them to stop offending and move in a healthy direction.

Ideally, Restorative Justice addresses the harms *caused by* and *revealed by* wrongdoing. Often wrongdoing is a symptom of some harm or a need in a person's life.

KO: Does RJ have a positive effect on crime prevention?

HZ: The research is generally quite positive about reduced recidivism for offenders who go through the process. They are less likely to repeat the crime. Schools are also finding that RJ has a lot of prevention potential. For example, a high school in Wellington, the capital of New Zealand, had a whole group of students who kept showing up in the courts. After they instituted a kind of Restorative Justice program in the schools, this cohort of "offenders" no longer showed up in the justice system. Issues were being resolved in the schools, students weren't getting in trouble, and they weren't being suspended.

Restoratively-oriented approaches are being used for workplace conflicts and harms, for example. Incorporating Restorative Justice into mediation in various contexts provides a way to address the issues of justice and injustice present in most conflicts, but often ignored by traditional mediation approaches.

What we are finding is when restorative discipline is used in schools—when, for example, circle processes are used to resolve issues—suspensions are reduced dramatically.

It is when students are suspended that they often get into more trouble. So to enhance prevention, you have to introduce restorative approaches in places like schools, and elsewhere in the community.

Restorative Justice does not offer a blueprint. Rather, it offers a compass. It points a direction and hopefully sparks a dialogue in each specific situation.

• • • • • • • • • •

Before the 2014 conference mentioned above, Katia (above right) and I were strolling through the market in Victoria, Tamaulipas, when we noticed two men following us. When we eventually confronted them, they said they were journalists, and they were certain I was Javier Sicilia, a famous Mexican poet and activist who had become the target of gangs because of his anti-gang activism after his son's violent death.

When we finally convinced them I was not, they wrote a story about Restorative Justice and my visit. Through our host, we were able then to meet with Mr. Sicilia (left above).

Mr. Sicilia was a friend of the famous philosopher Ivan Illich, and we met at Illich's home. In my blog I wrote, "By the time we said goodbye on the porch overlooking Illich's garden, even though we don't speak each other's language, I felt I had found a kindred spirit and friend."

. . . .

In the interview above I mention that Restorative Justice is applicable even without formal programs. I am inspired, for example, by my friends who are "restorative lawyers," bringing the philosophy to bear on the situations they encounter. Attorney Brenda Waugh describes it this way:

In my restorative practice of law, I try not to charge into developing a theory of the case, researching precedent for rights, or looking at sentencing guidelines. Instead, I stop and look at who is seated in front of me and explore how their experiences are impacting them? Are they afraid? Why? Do they fear loss? Has something damaged an important relationship? What can I do today and tomorrow to work to make right the wrongs? What can we do together to meet the needs of my client, and the opposing party, and the community? Can I create a collaborative environment to involve all of the stakeholders in working on meeting needs and healing the harm?

. . . .

I often say the "lens" of Restorative Justice is as important, and maybe more important, than specific programs.

"The promise and challenge of Restorative Justice" was the title of the introductory course I taught for many years at the Center for Justice and Peacebuilding. I wanted the participants in my classes to understand not only the meaning of Restorative Justice and the promises it offered, but also the difficulties and dangers involved. I sometimes said that I preferred skeptics to "true believers" who could envision no downsides.

As I mention above, Restorative Justice is easily misunderstood or misused. During one of my visits to Northern Ireland, there was a revenge shooting. A politician came on the radio proclaiming, "We have to stop this Restorative Justice." Hmm—not exactly what I have in mind for the term.

Another time, before the peace agreement there, my host and I met with a small paramilitary group who claimed to be doing Restorative Justice. As they explained their program, we asked what the role of the paramilitary was. "We do transportation," they said. We asked them to explain. "Well, if you were to go to the door and ask them to come to a victim offender conference, they'd say, 'F- off.' But if we come to the door, they'll say 'Let me get my shoes.'" There was no sense from them that the threat of violence might be inconsistent with RJ.

In a question-and-answer session at a conference in Russia, one participant asked me what our prosecutor said when we first introduced Restorative Justice. Reluctantly, I told him that I'd heard he proclaimed it a Communist plot. When the laughter died down, the questioner said, "Our prosecutor said it was a CIA plot!" We all laughed as we realized that we face similar challenges.

When receiving an invitation to speak somewhere, my wife Ruby always reminded me that it wouldn't end up being just one event. This became more challenging as I grew older. Here I am lecturing at the National Institute of Criminal Sciences (INACIPE), Mexico City, on the same trip as the above conference.

CHAPTER 2

Journey to Belonging:

What "victims" and "offenders" have in common

*T*hose who work in Restorative Justice are rightfully cautious about the terminology, "victim" and "offender," because of the simplistic way it labels people. I retain it here because it was in the original, but ask that readers keep this caution in mind.

I first made this presentation at a conference in New Zealand.

Recently I was given a challenging but rather risky assignment: to explore *at the same time* the "journey to belonging" that both victims and offenders must take. I found the assignment a fruitful challenge, but I must begin with two warnings:

- Some of you may find it problematic, even offensive, to address both victims and offenders together, and especially to assume there might be parallels or even intersections in their two journeys.

- At least some of what I say should be understood as exploratory and suggestive, rather than conclusive. I am on a journey here, too.

This topic and title, "Journey to Belonging," implies that alienation, as well as its opposite—belonging—are central issues for both those who offend and those who are offended against. The journey metaphor also suggests that the goal—belonging—requires a search or a process. Belonging is not simply that you either do or you don't. Instead, you might fall somewhere along a continuum.

The journey to belonging often involves a journey to identity. The two are deeply intertwined, like a double helix.

The journey to belonging and the journey to identity are journeys we all must make and then *remake*, not just victims and offenders. We make this journey as we move from childhood to adulthood, and sometimes we make parts of it again as we go through the stages of our lives. But when we experience insecure or traumatic or other life-changing situations, we often have to make these journeys anew, almost as if we were starting over.

Such journeys may be made along safe and healthy routes, but they can also be made along routes that are unhealthy. Racism, extreme nationalism, delinquent gangs, the conflicts we have seen in Northern Ireland or the former Yugoslavia, the process of "othering" that we do when we label offenders as outsiders—these are some of the sidetracks which occur when our desperate need to belong is resolved in unhealthy ways.

To explore this journey, I suggest we use the lenses of tragedy and of trauma. (When we use more common shorthand terms like "crime," we trigger a host of stereotypes and assumptions.) What these two ideas have in common is an experience of tragedy. The lens of tragedy may allow us to explore this reality with more empathy and understanding.

I will use the second experience—trauma—a bit loosely, as a continuum extending from very high levels of ordinary stress on one end, to traumatic and post-traumatic stress on the other. Such trauma is a core experience of both victims and offenders.

That victims of crime experience trauma is widely recognized—although the trauma of so-called "minor" crime is often overlooked.

What is less understood is that offenders often experience forms of trauma as well, both as a precursor to their offenses and as a result of their experience of "justice."

Much violence may actually be a reenactment of trauma that was experienced earlier but not responded to adequately. Unfortunately, society tends to respond by delivering more trauma in the form of imprisonment. Prisons, in fact, are some of the most powerful trauma factories I can imagine. While these realities must not be used to excuse, it is helpful to understand them, and they must be addressed.

Some years ago, I completed a book based on interviews with and photographs of men and women who were serving actual life sentences as a result of having participated in the taking of a life. A few years later I completed a similar project with survivors of severe violence. My conversations with those who have offended and those who have been offended against have convinced me that issues of belonging—of connection and disconnection—are intimately connected both to the *causes* of trauma and also to the *transcendence* of trauma. A core element of trauma is disconnection. The road to transcending trauma is through re-connection.

The journey to belonging often encompasses a number of "legs" or stretches along a route that often twists and turns, looping back on itself like a mountain road.

Journey toward meaning

Penny Beerntsen was attacked as she jogged on the beach, dragged into the woods, raped, beaten, and left for dead. In my book *Transcending: Reflections of Crime*

Victims, she compared her recovery or "re-ordering" to a jigsaw puzzle. There is more than one way to put the pieces together, she reflected, and the key is trying to find where the pieces fit.

Like many of the victims and survivors I have interviewed, Penny describes a world knocked out of alignment, logic destroyed. In this disordering lies one of the primary roots of trauma. When we become victims, the experience calls into question our most fundamental assumptions about who we are, who we can trust, and what kind of world we live in.

These include our assumptions about the orderliness of the world, our experience of autonomy or personal control, and our sense of relatedness—where we fit in a web of social relationships. Our lives rest on these three pillars. We built these pillars as we built our lives, from childhood to adulthood, and now they have been knocked out from under us.

The core trauma of victimization might be called the "three D's"—Disorder, Disempowerment, and Disconnection. So the journey from trauma to healing may mean revisiting issues we thought were long settled: Order, Empowerment, and Connection.

Paradoxically, offenders must travel a parallel road. I am convinced that offending behavior often arises out of unhealthy ways of coming to terms with these same "pillars." For a variety of reasons—one of which is trauma experienced as children—we may construct a world in which we establish a sense of Order based on violence and force, Empowerment by dominating others, and a sense of Connection rooted in kinship with fellow "outsiders" who also distrust others.

As with victims, the journey to healing for offenders means reconstituting these pillars, but in new ways. For offenders as well as victims, until these issues are settled, neither can belong. Since it involves relationships with others, the journey cannot be made alone.

Put another way, trauma involves the *destruction* of meaning. Transcendence of trauma involves the *recreation* of meaning. It is no accident that both victims and offenders who are on healing journeys have mentioned to me that Viktor Frankel's book, *Man's Search for Meaning*, based on his experience in the Holocaust, was important for them. In *Doing Life: Reflections of Men and Women Serving Life Sentences*, Tom Martin, who spent the rest of his life in prison because of a murder he committed, observed that a thinking person wants each day to matter, and one of the dilemmas is that too many lifers think. "So you face each day, not by saying, "How do I just struggle through?" but "What can I do to make something of this day?"

Penny Beerntsen, the survivor I cited earlier, describes the journey to belonging with a metaphor reminiscent of a looping mountain road, a chain of S-curves that seemed unconnected at first. The events she experienced appeared random, but then they seemed providentially connected. "It's like you start at the bottom. . . there's a curve, and you can't see what's at the end of that link. There are obstacles along the way. Then you get to the end, and Wow!, there's another link there. And you keep going."

Re-storying our lives

Our identities are embedded in our stories, so the re-creation of meaning requires "re-storying" our lives. Those who created the Truth and Reconciliation Commission in South Africa recognized that healing comes by facing one's past, coming to terms with it, drawing boundaries around it, and incorporating experiences of hurt and wrongdoing into a new story.

Repressed memories are dangerous. Painful experiences cannot be denied but must be incorporated into who we are. Sharon Wiggins was sentenced to death for a crime committed at age 13 or 14 and was given a life sentence. She knew she could not deny her violent and tragic past, even though it was difficult for her to believe she was now the same person. Yet she acknowledges that she wouldn't be the person she is today without those experiences.

Some time ago I met a man who had spent many years in prison. He had completed a master's degree and was now living successfully on the outside. Under his shirt he was wearing his prison t-shirt with his stenciled inmate number—so he would not forget where and who he had been.

For victims as well as offenders, this involves not only retelling their stories but transforming those stories of humiliation and shame into stories of dignity, courage, and honor. This process has a public as well as a private dimension. That's why Judith Lewis Herman, in her seminal book, *Trauma and Recovery*, prefers the term "testimony." Stories—or "testimonies"—are shaped in the telling and retelling. They need compassionate listeners to hear and to validate their "truths."

Journey toward judgment

For both victims and offenders, the journey toward meaning requires them to make moral judgments about what happened and their responsibility in it. Like it or not, they often find themselves struggling to understand and explain what happened in order to take an appropriate level of responsibility.

Victims tend to blame themselves, taking far too much responsibility for what went on. For them, a key need is to be vindicated. This includes acknowledging that a wrong was done to them and recognizing that someone else is responsible. That they are not ultimately to blame. Yet as Judith Herman has pointed out in *Trauma and Recovery*, most victims do not find it realistic to be totally absolved of all responsibility for what happened and/or how they responded to the trauma. Usually their process of recovery requires them to locate an appropriate spot somewhere between total responsibility and total blamelessness.

The same can be said for offenders who are on a healing path. They, too, must acknowledge those hurtful things that were done to them, while at the same time taking responsibility for the hurt they have caused. It is not healthy to rely on the traumas of one's past to explain away responsibility for wrongdoing. But neither can anyone be healthy without acknowledging and validating the harm they experienced.

Most offenders have been victims, or believe themselves to have been victims. Most violence is a response to a perceived violation. Violence—like the criminal justice system itself—is an effort to undo injustice. This sense of victimization may not be a valid excuse for victimizing others, but neither can it simply be ignored as if it did not exist or did not play a role.

Journey toward honor

A journey to meaning incorporates another journey—toward honor and respect. That brings us to the topic of shame and its close cousin, humiliation. We experience these as part of relating to others, so journeying toward honor is also intricately intertwined with the journey to belonging.

Shame is highly controversial within Restorative Justice circles. Many fear its misuse, and that it will be imposed rather than removed. Others, like my friend Rosemary Rowlands from the First Nations community in northern Canada, are convinced that their people have been so distorted by shame that they cannot imagine a positive use of the concept. Yet, while I acknowledge that is a legitimate concern, I am convinced that it is essential to explore this old and universal theme of shame.

However, I am coming to believe that humiliation—and its opposite, honor—continue to operate in powerful but often subterranean ways.

I am convinced that shame—along with the desire to avoid, remove, or transform it—motivates much, if not all, violence.

I suspect that shame is such a crucial component of victims' trauma that it drives and shapes their needs for justice.

Unfortunately, I also have no doubt that justice as we know it often does little to remove or transform shame, for either offender or victim. In fact, the process of justice often *increases* shame and humiliation for all parties. The result: offenders may re-offend and victims may demand vengeance.

In *Violence: Reflections on a National Epidemic*, James Gilligan argues that shame and the desire to remove it motivates much crime. If this is true, then our prescription for crime is bizarre: we impose more shame, stigmatizing offenders in ways that begin to define their identities and encourages them to join other "outsiders" in delinquent subcultures.

Guilt and shame become a self-perpetuating cycle, feeding one another.

Shame is ultimately ineffective as a deterrent to those at the fringes of society, such as racist groups or paramilitaries. Shame feeds rage cycles and forces those who are ostracized to come together more urgently. It often strengthens the very thing we hope to discourage. I remember vividly the reflections of a participant in one of my courses, a former paramilitary ex-prisoner in Northern Ireland. It was not shame that caused him to change—indeed, efforts at shame had strengthened his resolve and his solidarity with his compatriots. Instead, it was a new vision of meaning and belonging.

The experience of shame and humiliation is a thread that runs through victims' experiences as well. The struggle to remove or transform them is a central element in the journey to heal and belong. Why? Western society values power and autonomy, so it is shameful to be overpowered by others. When we are victimized, our status is lowered.

We are humiliated by the event itself, but also often by the ways we responded to it—the things we did or did not do at the time, the ways it affected us afterwards. Shame is further heaped on us when our versions of what happened are not validated by others, or when we are forced to keep our experiences secret.

But I have suspected that there is another layer to this as well. Ellen Halbert was brutally attacked in her bedroom by an enraged man in a Ninja suit who had hidden in her attic all night. When I interviewed her, she tied the sense of shame felt by victims to the fingers of *blame* pointed not only by others but by oneself.

Whether we have victimized or been a victim, the journey from brokenness and isolation to transcendence and belonging requires us to re-narrate our stories so that they are no longer just about shame and humiliation, but ultimately about dignity and triumph. Questions of meaning, honor, and responsibility are all part of this journey.

Journey toward vindication

The process of justice can contribute to or detract from this journey in a variety of ways. I want to explore just one of justice's important functions: vindication, to be cleared of blame and suspicion.

Violence itself is often driven by the needs to reciprocate, to vindicate oneself, to replace humiliation with honor. Both crime and justice often attempt to exchange humiliation for honor.

My work with victims suggests that the need for vindication is indeed one of the most basic needs that victims experience. It is one of the central demands that they make of a justice system. I believe, in fact, that this need for vindication is more basic and instinctual than the need for revenge. Revenge is but one among a number of ways that one can seek vindication.

What the victimizer has done, in effect, is to take his or her own shame and transferred it to the one victimized, lowering them in the process. When victims seek vindication from justice, in part they are seeking to throw back at their offender the shame and humiliation they've suffered.

By denouncing the wrong and establishing appropriate responsibility, the justice process should contribute to validating what's happened. But if we vindicate the victim by simply transferring that shame back to the offender, we are repeating and intensifying the cycle.

In order to progress on their journeys, *both* victim and offender need ways to replace their humiliation with honor and respect. Shame and humiliation must at least be removed and ideally be transformed. But this does not easily happen within the retribution framework of our current criminal justice systems.

Retribution or restoration?

Both retribution and restoration approaches to justice acknowledge a basic moral intuition that a balance has been thrown off by wrongdoing. Consequently, the victim deserves something, and the offender owes something. Both approaches agree that there must be a proportional relationship between the act and the response. Where they differ is on *what* will right the balance or acknowledge that reciprocity.

Retribution believes that pain will restore a sense of reciprocity. But the experience of shame and of trauma helps explain why this so often fails to achieve what is wished for by either victim or offender. Retribution as punishment seeks to vindicate and reciprocate, but it is often counterproductive.

Restorative Justice, on the other hand, says that what truly vindicates is to acknowledge a victim's harms and needs, combined with an active effort to encourage offenders to take responsibility, to make right the wrongs, and to address the causes of their behavior. By addressing this need for vindication in a positive way, Restorative Justice can affirm both victim and offender and help them transform their stories.

I have used the language of "humiliation" and "honor." We could use "disrespect" and "respect." The journey to belonging is also a journey from disrespect to respect. In fact, this journey to belonging is not just for victims and offenders, but for all of us.

Years ago I had the privilege of co-leading a retreat in a prison with Kathleen Denison, director of a non-profit working with incarcerated individuals. She noted that in the world of criminal justice, prison walls are overwhelming realities. Within those walls of concrete and razor ribbon we keep people locked up out of fear, pointing fingers of blame and shame, guarding others from them.

But the outer walls of prison are mirrored by inner prisons. Within each prisoner—and within each victim—within each one of us—there are parts of ourselves that we keep locked up and separated, pointing fingers of blame and shame, hiding these parts from others. All of us have traumas. All of us have inner wounds, parts of our personalities that we hide. We are apt to sentence these parts to life without parole. We all need healing.

Using retribution as a way to justice allows those walls to stand and grow thicker. The restorative approach is only possible when our wounds and traumas have been acknowledged. The outer world reflects the inner world. If we do not deal with our traumas, we are prone to reenact them. If our inner world is governed by fear, so is our worldview. If we maintain these inner walls, we cannot truly feel we belong.

How do we remove these walls? The biblical story of marching around the walls of Jericho, blowing horns until the walls fell, sounds dramatic but may be a tad impractical for many of us. Breaking them down seems too violent. Instead, this must be gentle work. We have to remove these walls tenderly, as the prophet Isaiah said when speaking of the Suffering Servant: ". . . a bruised reed he will not break, and a dimly burning wick he will not quench; he will faithfully bring forth justice."

The key is not in silencing the pain, reinforcing walls, and posting guards, but in giving voice to our pain and telling our truths. The solution is in what long-time peace advocate Elise Boulding calls "prophetic listening" to one another.

Crime is a symbol of our woundedness and alienation. So also is using retribution to find justice. The outer reality mirrors the inner reality. Only love and compassion can remove these walls. Only when these walls are addressed will we reach our destination. Only then will we belong.

• • • • • • • • • • •

I once spoke to a group that included a number of formerly incarcerated men and women. One man came up to me afterward and said, "Howard, that was a very interesting talk. Very interesting. However, I don't agree with any of it."

I would guess that his reaction was in part evidence of what those who research shame tell us about Western culture: that we are ashamed of shame. We don't talk about it and in fact don't even have a language for it. As a result, they say, shame has gone underground, cropping up in unfortunate ways. Some, for example, attribute Americans' obsession with wealth to this phenomenon.

• • • • • • • • • • •

Years ago I offered a seminar on shame in our graduate program. The format was that we would read literature on shame, then meet over lunch to discuss it. The conversations were deeply personal; I was moved by how deep the feelings were and how pervasive the impact of shame was on the participants' lives.

. . . .

In 2000, I was invited to give a series of lectures at a Restorative Justice conference in Dzerzhinsk, Russia. For one of the sessions, they asked me to speak about shame. I thought it a strange request for an introductory Restorative Justice conference, but complied. It turned out to be a pivotal point in the conference.

This conference brought people from the newly-established profession of social work together with members of law enforcement. Relations between them had been tense during the conference. At the end of the lecture, social workers began to accuse the police of shaming and disrespecting the clients—especially children—they worked with. The police began to talk about how they were being shamed by officials above them, including judges. Suddenly they had shared experiences and began to talk with each other. The whole tenor of the conference changed.

I am convinced that the topics of shame and of honor deserve much more attention in research and in our daily lives.

. . . .

Those Russian trips bring back memories:

Twice on trips to Russia I was asked by the non-profit I was working with to carry $10,000 in cash to Russia to replenish their operating funds. This was before the banking system was working there so that other alternatives for transferring funds to their programs were unavailable.

With Russian colleague Rustem Maksudov
at Red Square in Moscow.

Before I went the first time, I received an email saying I was to carry 10 boxes of chocolate pudding. Someone has a real obsession, I thought, and was about to purchase the pudding when I got a message that this was code for cash.

I landed in Ukraine, only to learn that I had to carry the cash on an overnight train to Moscow.

The second time, I flew directly into Moscow, again carrying $10,000 in $20 bills. No one I recognized was there to meet me at the airport, but a taxi driver was holding a sign with what could have been construed as my name. With some trepidation, I got into his cab. As we drove through Moscow, I was relieved when I recognized that the neighborhood we were entering was one I had been to on my previous visit.

Signing books at the release of the Russian version of my book, *Changing Lenses*. The translator commented that the translation was quite a challenge because it drew from so many different disciplines.

CHAPTER 3

Good Intentions
Aren't Enough

This topic hasn't often been well received by Restorative Justice practitioners. I recall a talk I gave on the topic at an early RJ conference; it was one of the most hostile audiences I have faced. But it is critically important, as I say in this entry from the blog I maintained for several years.

Cell, Eastern State Penitentiary

Some time ago my daughter and I walked through the Eastern State Penitentiary in Philadelphia, now a museum. Eastern State Penitentiary was the beginning of the modern prison or penitentiary. It was built in the early 1800s with great hopes and much fanfare—an alternative to the prevailing practices of corporal and capital punishment. People came from all over the world to see and copy this wonderful phenomenon. De Tocqueville, the great commentator on the new American democracy, actually came to America primarily to observe the prison.

In spite of their good intentions, the Quakers and others who invented the prison had created a monster. In fact, pressures for reform began almost immediately. Important lessons are to be found here. Reforms and innovations often have unintended consequences. Even with the best intentions, social change efforts can and will go astray.

But there is another, perhaps more fundamental, lesson from the birth of prisons: what seems good for me may not be good for others. Research into the social circumstances of early prison advocates reveals that some of the Quaker promoters of penitentiaries had themselves been imprisoned for conscience's sake. Because they were men of substance, they were not treated as badly as they would have been otherwise. Because they were men of reflection, they found their incarceration to be a time for contemplation. Consequently, they advocated prison as a place to reflect on the Bible and become penitent. Unfortunately, what was liberating for them soon became oppressive to others.

This is an important warning for those of us who advocate for Restorative Justice and, in fact, any social change. Our visions may reflect class, gender, religious, and cultural biases—and they may be fundamentally flawed. To guard against this, we need to be self-critical, to open ourselves to evaluation and feedback. We need to create space to hear from divergent and diverse voices.

In short, we must practice the accountability we espouse for others.

* * * * * * * * * * *

Having been trained as an historian (my Ph.D. is in European history), I researched the history of criminal justice reform in the U.S. while developing the RJ concept. What I found was sobering. So-called reforms often turned out to be much different than intended, and sometimes worse than the problem they were trying to fix.

In the early days of victim-offender conferencing, for example, one state department of corrections was using victim-offender meetings basically as a way to punish offenders. Instead, these meetings should be used to empower both those who have been harmed and those who caused harm.

As I often told my students, all social interventions, no matter how well intended, have unintended consequences. All will be co-opted and misused. It is our responsibility as advocates and practitioners to be alert to this.

Changing the lens of a camera, mounting a wide-angle instead of a telephoto lens: only a photographer could use this kind of metaphor well in the debate on "doing justice!" Howard showed that many things can change if we learn to frame facts, so that they can also reveal the broader contours, the field in which they lie.

We can say that by considering precise facts of evil we can mount different lenses, which are not mutually exclusive, but which can help us to respond to evil with greater respect for all people, truly succeeding—almost as artisans of peace—in putting things right.

I met Howard in Trieste. He agreed to speak at some events on Restorative Justice, and so many of us eagerly awaited his visit to Italy. There is a photo in which I portrayed him on the Molo Audace, at the city seafront. And I keep a photo that Howard took of me.

There are friends who exchange books; others who exchange photographic portraits. I am very grateful that Howard is not only on the shelves of my library, but also in the family album!

—*Giovanni Grandi, University of Trieste, Italy*

CHAPTER 4

The Promise and the Challenge of Restorative Justice for Victims

(with Mary Achilles)

*V*ictim advocates have often been very skeptical about Restorative Justice, and for good reason. I share some of their concerns and have made it a priority to remind the Restorative Justice field of them.

I was honored to co-author this chapter with Mary Achilles, who at that time was the Governor of Pennsylvania's Victim Advocate, the only Governor-appointed and legislatively-approved victim advocate in the United States. Mary often said that she was a better advocate for victims because of Restorative Justice.

I appreciated the way Mary combined a critical stance toward Restorative Justice alongside her support for it. It was under Mary's leadership that the Office of the Victim

Advocate initiated a program for a victim-initiated victim-offender dialogue program for situations where the one who caused harm was in prison. This program became a model for other states.

Rarely does the Western process of justice deliver good news for crime victims. A leading specialist on trauma, Judith Lewis Herman, has stated it plainly in her book, *Trauma and Recovery*: "If one set out to design a system for provoking intrusive, post-traumatic symptoms, one could not do better than a court of law."

For the majority of victims, "justice" remains an unsavory and unsatisfactory experience.

Perhaps the boldest initiative to address the roles of victims in justice within the modern era is the Restorative Justice movement—and its position that the definition of justice underlying the Western legal system is itself flawed.

Restorative Justice seeks to refocus the conception of and approach to justice so that harms to victims is central to the definition of, and response to, crime. But *can* Restorative Justice deliver this to victims? Is it likely to do so? What are the possibilities and challenges?

Since Restorative Justice approaches often operate within the traditional, offender-oriented justice system, many are concerned that restorative approaches will be distorted in such a way that victims will once again be sidelined or misused. These dangers are magnified by naiveté on the part of some Restorative Justice practitioners and by failures to fully implement restorative values within this movement.

At least four factors may contribute to the failures of Restorative Justice to live up to its promise:

1. As Restorative Justice has become more popular, it has often been viewed as a program or methodology, rather than a philosophy with a set of underlying values and principles.

   As a concept, Restorative Justice places great emphasis on the roles and needs of victims and addresses offender accountability first of all in terms of the harm done to the victim.

   However, many programs have not adopted an explicit statement on values and philosophy. Without that framework, and the benchmarks of good practice they imply, an offender-orientation will almost certainly be perpetuated.

2. The focus on Restorative Justice as a methodology has been compounded by a tendency to assume that "one size fits all," rather than to have program shapes emerge out of community dialogues about values, philosophy, needs, and resources.

3. Organizers of Restorative Justice programs have commonly failed to include victim voices early on in the

design and implementation of programs. Without these voices at the table, it is unlikely that victim interests and concerns will be addressed. Moreover, once the program is underway, it is unrealistic to assume that victim and victim advocates will join in with a full sense of ownership and engagement if they have not been there from the start.

4. Restorative Justice programs have failed to build in— and sometimes have even been hostile to—evaluation, especially the kind that assesses practice and outputs against values, mission, and philosophy.

An important safeguard against having Restorative Justice subverted and coopted is to insist on an ongoing emphasis on its principles and values. This means that whenever it moves from the visionary to the implementation stage, it must find ways to balance attention to practice with attention to principles. What is always needed is an ongoing emphasis on value-based practice.

Essential also are efforts to create a much fuller dialogue between victims and ex-offenders, victim advocates and service providers, offender advocates and service providers, and Restorative Justice advocates and practitioners.

To address the concern about victims specifically, we propose the following guidelines or signposts for practicing Restorative Justice.

We are working toward appropriate victim involvement in Restorative Justice programs when:

1. *Victims and victim advocates are represented on governing bodies and initial planning committees.*
   When they are included in the process of developing and managing programs, their presence highlights the programs' commitment to crime victims and the sensitivities that need to be addressed so as not to revictimize. Victims and their advocates are unusually suited to offer the subtleties of program design that ensure safe and welcoming messages to injured crime victims.

2. *Efforts to involve victims grow out of a desire to assist them, not offenders.* Victims are not responsible to rehabilitate or assist offenders unless they choose to do so.
   In most cases, the present system of justice is fundamentally a business, designed for processing offenders. The concern for offenders is important, but we must be careful never to use victims primarily as a way to benefit or otherwise deal with offenders. That should not be the reason for victim involvement in justice.

3. **Victims' safety is a fundamental element of program design.**
   Whether working with crime victims in the immediate aftermath of an incident, or years later, all

interventions must first and foremost recognize the victim's safety and security needs, both physical and emotional, as articulated by them. Victims must be free to express their natural human responses to the crime, including anger, rage, and need for vengeance without judgment and with understanding of their pain.

4. *Victims clearly understand their roles in the program, including potential benefits and risks to themselves and offenders.*

Victims must be prepared for participating in the program by giving them as much information as possible about their role in the process, what to expect, and the known risks and benefits to themselves and to offenders. Victims should be informed of any benefits to the offender through the program.

5. *Confidentiality is provided within clear guidelines.*

A victim's right to privacy must always be protected. Victims should choose when, what, and how information is disclosed about them and their experience. They should also be informed of any rules and regulations regarding confidentiality under which the program operates.

6. ***Victims are given as much information as possible about their case, the offense, and the offender.***

Victims may or may not choose to engage in face-to-face dialogue with the offender, or there may be other reasons why it is inappropriate or impractical for the victim and offender to meet. Still, victims usually want information about the offender, and that can and should be addressed.

7. ***Victims can identify and articulate their needs and are given choices.***

The opportunity to identify their own needs and make choices about how they are addressed can help to re-empower victims. Certainly, victims must be the gatekeepers as to whether and when a direct encounter with their offenders takes place.

Early on, before the program I (Howard) was directing was taking non-property cases, a woman who had been victim of a rape came to us and asked to meet with the man who did it. I visited the man in prison, but he declined to participate. However, I had taken a list of her questions, and he was willing to answer them, at least to some extent. Even though it went no further, the woman reported that this helped her move forward.

8. *Victims' opportunities for involvement are maximized.*

Since a core element of victim trauma is disempowerment, Restorative Justice programs should provide as many opportunities as possible for victims to be involved in their cases, as well as the program as a whole.

9. *Program design provides referrals for additional support and assistance.*

Crime victims may have additional needs that cannot be met by the program. Programs ought to be familiar with additional community services for victims and routinely make those referrals.

10. *Services are available to victims even when their offenders have not been arrested or are unwilling or unable to participate.*

If victims are central to the process of justice, and their needs are the starting point, then as a justice system we cannot simply offer services only when an offender is identified and/or arrested. To the extent possible, we must provide services and options for victims when the offender is not known.

Conclusion

For Restorative Justice to live up to its claims, it must remain grounded in principle. It must not only listen to victims' voices, but also incorporate them.

Restorative Justice offers a hopeful vision of justice for victims, but good intentions and wonderful ideas are not enough. Substantial challenges must be met if this vision is to prove a reality rather than a mirage.

> Sometimes those who have been harmed may find it helpful to meet with surrogates—people who have committed harms similar to what they have experienced.
>
> In a case of murder by a family member, the sister was not ready to meet with her brother who committed the murders. Instead, she asked if she could accompany me (Howard) to prison to meet with a group of men I was working with who had themselves been involved in homicides.
>
> We sat in a circle, and she asked if each man would be willing to say what happened in his case, and to imagine what might have led her brother to do what he did. Respectfully, each one did so, leading to a powerful dialogue. She later expressed much appreciation for this.

* * * * * * * * * * *

As one way to address these concerns, some years ago a group of us conducted a "listening project." We sent teams made up of one RJ advocate and one victim advocate to a number of states where we knew there were tensions and/ or misunderstandings between Restorative Justice practitioners and victim service providers. These teams were trained and tasked to listen to victim advocates with a series of open-ended questions.

The responses were compiled, and after an in-person consultation involving representatives from each group and state, a report was published. Restorative Justice groups were encouraged to do similar listening projects in their communities as a way of holding themselves accountable and building bridges.

The report, entitled "A Listening Project: Taking Victims and Their Advocates Seriously," by Harry Mika, Mary Achilles, Ellen Halbert, Lorraine Stutzman Amstutz, and Howard Zehr, is available on various websites and expands on the concerns and suggestions in the above article.

. . . .

For three years I served on the Victim Advisory Group of the U.S. Sentencing Commission that establishes and oversees guidelines for federal judges. I was struck by how little concern for victims' needs and wishes was evident in the guidelines. A Restorative Justice perspective would have provided some correctives and options, but as that did not seem to be possible, I left after my term was up.

. . . .

The system's unresponsiveness to the needs and wishes of victims was starkly illustrated for me years ago when I was contacted by the daughter of a murdered police officer with a request to meet the man who committed the crime before he was executed, which she opposed. There was no program for this in the state where this case occurred, and those of us working on it were stymied at every turn.

I met with the man who was condemned to die, and he was willing to meet. But the Department of Corrections informed us that they knew that this was not good for victims. We even appealed to the governor, with no success.

Finally, shortly before the execution, the lawyers working on the case arranged for the woman to travel to their office, and the victim and the offender were able to talk by phone in 15-minute segments. Later she told me that she was grateful for even this limited exchange.

CHAPTER 5

Justice as Art,
Art as Justice

This chapter is adapted from a presentation at the Arts & Criminal Justice Symposium sponsored by the Mural Arts Program (MAP), Philadelphia. What cannot be conveyed here, unfortunately, are the images accompanying the talk or the musical exploration of restorative justice through drumming led by musicians Frances Crowhill Miller and Daryl Snider.

MAP uses art—especially murals—to empower and rebuild community and has integrated Restorative Justice principles into their philosophy. I have had the privilege of working with them on a number of projects.

For the past five decades I have worked mostly in the criminal justice arena. However, I am also a serious photographer, having worked professionally as an international photojournalist, and I continue to pursue documentary, portrait, and landscape photography. My challenge has been to find ways to bring together these two areas of work, these two worlds, these two parts of my brain.

Part of the problem is that the predominant "ways of knowing" in criminal justice (and in academics, where I have spent years) are directly opposite to art. The worlds of justice and of academics both emphasize rational, analytic, and verbal approaches and are skeptical of more intuitive, emotional, and less linear approaches. Justice relies heavily on methods that are conflictual and adversarial. In academics, knowledge is often thought to emerge from critique and debate.

An American Correctional Association film designed to orient employees portrays the American criminal justice system as a boxing match between professionals who stand in for the defendant and the state, refereed by a judge. Note that the victim is missing from this metaphor. In many jurisdictions, outcomes are guided by supposedly rational and also mathematical sentencing guidelines that leave limited room for intuition or even judgment.

I have attempted to bring together my two areas of interest by using my photographic and artistic interests in the service of justice. This has forced me to rethink some assumptions about justice and about academics.

I am convinced that if done respectfully and responsibly, photography, and the arts in general, have tremendous potential to build bridges between people, to encourage mutual understanding, and to nurture healthy dialogue. For example, in my book, *Doing Life: Reflections of Men*

& Women Serving Life Sentences, I try to portray life-sentenced prisoners as human beings who are much more than the worst thing they have ever done.

Respectful photographic portraits that avoid common stereotypes, combined with these lifers' own words, challenge the reader/viewer to listen to real people instead of the simplistic, stereotyped conversations about justice that are so common. The resulting conversations which I've had, and the responses I have received from many people, even including crime victims, suggests that this has been successful.

In two later books—*Transcending: Reflections of Crime Victims* and *What Will Happen to Me?*—I seek to do the same for victims of crime and for children who have parents in prison.

I once received a report about a woman on a jury who refused to vote for a life sentence. When asked why, she said that her husband had given her a copy of *Doing Life* for Christmas and, after seeing these people and reading their stories, she could not vote for this sentence.

Underlying this kind of work are two fundamental premises. First, artistic ways of knowing, communicating, collaborating, and being have immense power. Much of our learning comes through visuals. To rely primarily on words is to drastically limit our capacity to communicate. What's more, the arts generally—sound, as well as visual—have enormous potential to engage the whole person emotionally and intuitively, as well as rationally.

The arts can also engage and empower those whose strengths may not be in words or who may not have a way to speak clearly. They can create safe spaces to explore, to experiment, and to talk about painful and difficult subjects. Very importantly, the arts allow for multiple interpretations. They reflect the ambiguity, the paradox, and the complexity that we all experience, a reality that is often not recognized in our criminal justice system.

The second fundamental premise underlying this work for me is that art, and life, must be grounded in a relational and whole-person concept of justice. Genuine justice is about acknowledging the humanity of *all*, about healing harms and acknowledging relationships. And that brings me to Restorative Justice.

I've been pleased to learn that all three of these books have been used in prison settings. Incarcerated individuals have reported that *Transcending* has helped them understand the perspective of victims. Some youth facilities have used *Doing Life* to help young people think about the impact of their actions. *What Will Happen to Me?* provides a way for parents in prison to understand their children's experiences.

As I've noted, Restorative Justice seeks to reframe the way we conventionally think about wrongdoing and justice—away from our preoccupation with lawbreaking, guilt, and punishment, toward a focus on harms, needs, and obligations. Restorative Justice especially emphasizes the importance of engaging and empowering those most affected by wrongdoing and takes a problem-solving approach. It can be viewed in part as a needs-based understanding of justice, in contrast with the what-one-deserves-based approach of the Western legal model.

I believe that Restorative Justice reflects three basic assumptions:

1. Crime is a violation of people and relationships.

2. Violations create obligations.

3. The central obligation is to put right the wrongs.

Translated into a set of principles, Restorative Justice calls us to:

1. Focus on the harms and consequent needs of the victims, as well as the communities' and the offenders'.

2. Address the obligations that result from those harms, the obligations of offenders, as well as the communities' and society's.

3. Use inclusive, collaborative processes as much as possible.

4. Involve those with a legitimate stake in the situation, including victims, offenders, community members, and society, in deciding what to do.

5. Seek to put right the wrongs as much as possible.

This approach to justice is grounded in the reality that we depend on others and they depend on us. Our actions affect others, and their actions affect us. Consequently, it is important to expand our connections and reduce "othering" and social distance.

Part of what makes it possible for our society to be so punitive is that the less we know people as real people, the more we tend to "other" them (or see them in stereotyped terms as different from us), and so the easier it is to punish. This is what makes possible our massive incarceration in the United

Since this presentation was given, the COVID pandemic has given a new meaning to the term "social distance." Here and elsewhere I am using the term as used by Nils Christie and others, referring to *relational* distance, not physical distance. Social distance in this sense has to do with the extent with which we can identify and empathize with others. In the remainder of this book I will use the term "relational social distance" to differentiate it from the pandemic use of the term.

States and what allows us to pursue our foreign wars against "the enemy."

"Othering" is key to the way race is constructed in our society, and criminal justice is deeply implicated in this, continuing to reflect and contribute to "othering." This is clear in the racial and ethnic makeup of mass incarceration. The way both victims and offenders are often portrayed in the media helps to create the sense of social apartness that makes these policies palatable. In fact, as I noted earlier, even the terms "victim" and "offender" encourage othering. Whether implicitly or explicitly, this social apartness serves as a tool of social control.

Prisoner photographs often contribute to this. Most photographs of prisoners, if not unflattering mug shots, focus on the bizarre and foreboding character of the prison environment: bars, cells, tattoos. For viewers who have not personally experienced these settings, the portrayals engender a sense of danger and difference. So in my *Doing Life* project, I deliberately deprived viewers of these stereotypic triggers, hoping that readers would engage with the images and words of lifers as real individuals, worth knowing and taking seriously.

Photography also has a long history of helping to construct Native American racial and ethnic identities in mainstream American society. These constructions have ranged from a people who need to be conquered and "civilized," to the "noble savage." Many times this construction of Native Americans as the "other" has been intentional.

Our "ways of knowing" in research and in journalism continue to contribute to this. We so often see our "subjects" as objects to be used as we see fit. The author is the expert, the authority, the owner, and supposedly the objective arbiter of knowledge. Much journalism and research has tended to focus on our differences rather than our common humanity.

In fact, the words "research," "journalism," and even "justice" have often been connected to conquering impulses and action. It is no accident that New Zealand's youth justice system, perhaps the world's first legal system organized around a Restorative Justice style conference, resulted in part from the indigenous Maori's critique that the Western legal system was both culturally inappropriate and a form of institutional racism.

So Restorative Justice requires a re-thinking of our assumptions, our "ways of knowing," whether in justice or in research, journalism. . . or art. It encourages us to:

- respect our "subjects" or "clients," our "co-workers" or "colleagues," treating them as collaborators and co-creators;
- recognize that the process may be as important as the product or end result;

- acknowledge the limits and subjectivity of what we "know";
- be aware of the power dynamics at play in our interactions;
- and realize that all of this is less about our uniqueness as authors, artists, and justice workers than about finding ways to bring us together as a human family.

The bottom line, for me, is that real justice is as much an art as a science. It must involve the *whole* person, and artistic ways of knowing are essential to this. I am drawn to thinking of the justice practitioner as an artist.

Restorative Justice relies heavily on dialogue, communication, imagination, creativity, and intuition. Artistic ways of knowing can contribute to understanding and to conversation. They can help to reduce "othering," while at the same time providing opportunities to explore the realities of lived experience.

Of course there is a place for science and the rational. Neuroscientist Dan Siegel, in a recent lecture at our university, called for us to be "scientifically consistent but not scientifically constrained."

As we work in the justice arena, as we seek to improve the experience of crime victims while reducing our reliance on prison—as we use the arts in this process—it is important to be grounded in a vision of how we want to live together in this world. Remember these values as the "three R's"—respect, responsibility, and relationships. But I also emphasize two more that are especially relevant here. One of these is *humility*. Humility is not only about what we take credit for or how we act—humility is about who we are and what we know.

All of us are shaped by our history, our culture, our gender, our ethnicity, our biographies. This is a source of our strength and uniqueness as individuals, but it also a limitation. My experience as a White graduate of Morehouse College, an historically Black college—then as a professor at Talladega College, another historically Black college—affected me profoundly. I became acutely aware that I speak as an American male of European ancestry and Mennonite cultural and religious background, no matter how conscious I am of these advantages and how much I try to overcome them. With them come certain strengths and privileges. With them also come a whole set of blinders. I must be endlessly cautious about generalizing what I "know" to other people and situations, or imposing my views on others.

Only with a deep appreciation for and openness to others' realities can we live together in a restorative way. This means that listening and dialogue are essential for art and for justice.

Another value or attitude has become central to me: an attitude of *wonder* or *awe*. As one of my early professors said during the first days of a philosophy class, we in the West have been shaped by the approach of the philosopher Descartes: an attitude of doubt or skepticism. That will not be our approach in this study of philosophy, the professor announced. Rather, we will be informed by *wonder and awe* at the possibilities of this universe and the human mind.

David James Duncan, in his book *My Story as Told by Water*, provides a powerful definition of wonder: "... wondering is unknowing, experienced as pleasure." In the arts and in justice we have a great deal of pleasure ahead.

Respect, responsibility, relationships, humility, wonder. These are foundational values for those who seek justice and art that heals and restores. They are key values for justice and art on the healing edge.

* * * * * * * * * * *

Although a major concern in my work has been to challenge stereotypes, this wasn't apparent from my first two academic publications. My first book, "Crime and the Development of Modern Society," featured a gruesome engraving of a mother strangling her child—even though that was not relevant to the topic. Happily, that book has recently been re-issued without that cover image. My next publication was in a chapter in a Belgian journal with a cover depicting beheaded bodies hanging upside down. Fortunately, that trend of gory images stopped there.

. . . .

In 2007 I was part of a "visual restoration" project at the Mural Arts Program. Entitled the Albert M. Greenfield Restorative Justice Program, it was intended to help a group of youth who were serving day detention sentences to give back and re-connect to their community. I was asked to do photographic portraits of "cultural elders" from this diverse community.

After training in interviewing and writing, the young people interviewed these elders, and then created a variety of verbal and visual explorations including exhibits and murals. It was gratifying to be part of this imaginative and practical blend of art and justice.

. . . .

On the very day I was editing this chapter for the book, I was reminded of my Morehouse College experience when I received a surprise call from Rev. Ronald English, one of my Morehouse classmates. I had not been in touch with him for over 50 years, but I immediately remembered that it was he who had introduced me to Dr. Martin Luther King, Jr. on the steps behind the pulpit at Ebenezer Baptist

Church in Atlanta. Ronald is a pastor, now involved in Restorative Justice, and had recently learned from another Morehouse graduate of my involvement in the field. I love these connections.

. . . .

Helping to make connections has been a source of great satisfaction to me throughout my career. It is very rewarding to connect people with similar interests and concerns to others who share those interests. Recently, for example, I was being interviewed by a Ph.D. candidate who, I discovered, had a background in photography. We discussed ways that she might use her photography in pursuit of her justice interests, and I connected her to one of our "students"—a professional photographer using photography to connect Palestinian and Israeli women. I later learned that they were planning to lead a workshop together. What a joy!

In the early 1990s, I was asked by Mennonite Central Committee to produce a book that would celebrate its 75th anniversary. It was to feature portraits of local partners around the world, along with interviews about their dreams for their lives and families. I did the portraits and interviews with Palestinians on the West Bank, then commissioned photographers to go elsewhere. Here I am meeting with Mother Theresa, asking her to write a forward to the book, entitled *A Dry Roof and a Cow*. Eventually she declined, citing her work schedule, but I was honored to meet her.

While I'm name-dropping: In 1985, while serving as chair
of the National Coalition to Abolish the Death Penalty,
I wrangled an audience with Pope John Paul II to ask
him to intervene in a pending death penalty situation.
He ultimately declined, saying he could not interfere in
the affairs of another country. However, soon after that
he did begin to intervene in other cases. My wife Ruby
thinks maybe we helped soften him up. She also says that
in this photo I look like I am trying to sell him a used car.

The first time I met Howard, he happened to mention that he was a Morehouse College graduate (I later found out that he was the first white man to graduate from this historically black institution). At that time, I had no idea about Howard's significance in the Restorative Justice movement but, as a Black woman who grew up in an HBCU community, I wanted to know about his time at Morehouse!

As an RJ practitioner, I developed a deep appreciation for Howard's writings. I am certain his words on Restorative Justice will guide the careers of future generations, as well.

—*Sheryl Wilson, executive director, Kansas Institute for Peace and Conflict Resolution, Bethel College, North Newton, KS*

When I first read one of Prof. Howard's books, I found many similarities with my indigenous system Jirga.

The next day I went straight to his office to discuss. Prof. Howard encouraged me to take his RJ class, and the journey started.

—*Ali Gohar, Swabi, Khyber Pukhtoon Khawa, Pakistan*

In order to understand a certain social movement, you need to comprehend the original vision and history of the movement.

This book is about the what, why, who, and how of Restorative Justice. "The Grandfather of Restorative Justice," Dr. Zehr, gently recounts to us his personal, social, and spiritual journey.

As his former student, I admire Dr. Zehr, not only for his teaching and guidance, but also for his devotion and humility in pioneering a new paradigm and new practices. His work and legacy will be carried on by his comrades and followers around the world, including myself.

—*Jae Young Lee, director of Korea Association for Restorative Justice, Gyunggido, South Korea*

I loved this book, a summation of Howard Zehr's life's work, developing a truly revolutionary movement. It has given me a vision as a lawyer/mediator about how to practice justice—but also, as a human being, how to live restoratively.

Howard is the "Real Deal"—he returns phone calls from a campsite in Canada, is always open to critique, and wary of unintended consequences; he lives as a photographer with wonder and awe, with an earthy sense of humor (which got me through Covid), and he drinks espresso while communicating with Morse Code!

—*Tom Porter, lawyer, teacher, minister, mediator, Wellesley, MA*

This is a great book for anywhere, because it tells you things you didn't know about Howard and about Restorative Justice. It gets even seasoned practitioners of RJ thinking!

Howard's contribution to thinking and learning about justice issues can't be overstated. It is immense.

Following an early visit of Howard's to Aotearoa, New Zealand, I wrote that we saw him as a "prophet of justice," a term that I meant in both religious and non-religious senses. That is even more true now that I have read this book and seen what he has done with his "retirement." Such a word doesn't seem to apply.

He has been on a continuous curve of teaching and mentoring. Well done, Howard!

—*Fred McElrea, former district judge and academic, New Zealand*

In 2008, Howard generously agreed to travel to Denmark to speak at a hearing on victim offender mediation at The Danish Parliament.

Many were new to the ideas of Restorative Justice, and Howard spoke to the large, inquisitive audience in his always gentle, inspiring, and encouraging way.

To this day, almost 15 years later, I still meet people who tell me that it was then that the notion of Restorative Justice became comprehensible to them.

—*Karin Sten Madsen, RJ practitioner, Copenhagen, Denmark*

Intellectual honesty, conceptual clarity, integration of fields of knowledge and talents that allowed Restorative Justice to surpass the frontiers of criminal justice, and empower and encourage justice professionals in foreign cultures — these are a few of the unique traits of Professor Howard Zehr.

Rarely do we encounter such powerful capacity to transform worldviews, institutions, legal procedures, curricula, communities, and the lives of thousands of people.

As a human being, he embodies the values of Restorative Justice, which we today acknowledge as a philosophy and an art of living.

—*Lia Diskin, co-founder of Associação Palas Athena, Brazil*

Nearly 40 years ago, as a young Black man growing up in the shadow of Rikers Island, I first encountered Howard Zehr when I was a college transfer student. All these years later, I am now a professor of religion and African & African American Studies.

I found this book inspiring. But the thing that truly enlivens it are the narratives of human striving toward justice to which Zehr testifies by way of the all-too-human stories he tells and the living portraits often accompanying them.

Howard has a scientific and artful heart, deeply determined to imagine the human condition beyond retribution—indeed, striving (*as much as possible*) to "put things right" for victims, holding offenders accountable within inclusive communities of restorative care for all persons impacted by wrongdoing.

—*James S. Logan, Earlham College*

My peers and I somehow always felt trusted by Howard. This was not because of traits of ours, but instead because of his unique ability to see the best in people, and to gently and graciously bestow upon those around him the responsibility of leadership.

His innate trust in others led us to trust ourselves — what a gift!

—*Aaron Lyons, Just Outcomes*

I was privileged to be one of Howard's students and to get to know him and work with him closely.

He's an amazing scholar with beautiful human qualities (humility, a sense of humor, respect, a great listener, community connector, etc.)

I define myself as a Restorative Justice practitioner.

—*Najla El Mangoush, Foreign Minister, Libya*

In lieu of a conventional autobiography, this is the closest we can come to Howard Zehr talking about himself.

Who is he? A person, a journey, a teacher, a pilgrim, a sceptic, a mystic, and a scholar—who has ever so gently upended the dominant paradigms of the modern criminal justice system.

A visually delectable, lucid recount that can be heard and conversed with, it fills up one's senses with the beauty of a life lived in wonder.

—*Rina Kashyap, University of Delhi, New Delhi, India*

This book is excellent.

One of Howard's strengths, in spite of his world-renowned work, is to not make the story of Restorative Justice about himself.

So, I find it exciting to see some of the "story of Howard" in this book—how his generosity, kindness, critical thinking, clear communication, and willingness to be accountable have shaped the movement known as Restorative Justice.

Worth reading!

—*Judah Oudshoorn, Conestoga College, Kitchener, ON*

I appreciate the insight and reflection that Howard brings to looking at earlier writings — seeing what is unchanging and what is evolving as we learn more about ourselves and each other and the possibilities of a non-Western world view.

—*Kay Pranis, circle trainer, author*

 CONTINUED ON PAGE 118—

PART 2

How I Got Here, Personally

CHAPTER 6

How I Got Here

A conversation with
Bruna Pali

Brunilda Pali is a professor at Leuven Institute of Criminology in Belgium with a special interest in feminism, critical social theory, social justice, Restorative Justice, and arts. I have had the privilege of interacting with her on several projects. We had the following conversation for her internet blog, "Restorotopias."

Brunilda Pali:. Howard, your work has had a major influence in the development of Restorative Justice, perhaps even more than you intended. Can you go back in time to your first moment of encounter with the restorative spirit and ideas and tell us about it? What was your drive, what were your concerns, what were you reacting to, what were you hoping to create?

Howard Zehr: When I first rolled out the idea of Restorative Justice, I expected it to be dismissed as a bit crazy. My main goal at that point was to write something provocative.

It's hard to say where the "restorative spirit" came from. I'm sure much of it initially had to do with the values inherent in my Anabaptist faith tradition. After my first year in college, I decided to leave the safety of my community and push myself, while hoping to understand justice issues more deeply. So in 1963, in my sophomore year, I entered Morehouse College, an historically Black college. That was a formative experience.

After my graduate studies, between 1971-78, I taught at Talladega College, another historically Black institution. There I got involved with the realities of justice by working with prisoners and with defense attorneys who were working on death penalty, prison riot, and police brutality cases.

I was inspired by the spirit of Norwegian criminologist Nils Christie's little book, *Limits to Pain*, that I viewed as a "provocative essay." It challenged some basic assumptions about punishment and was important for my thinking.

A faculty colleague, Bernie Bray, and I led teams of Talladega students to find out what we could about people listed as potential jurors on cases. The defense team would use this information in selecting a jury. To do this, we had to network in communities and interview people who might know people on the list. Although I had learned to network earlier—often around my electronics interests—this is where I learned to interview.

I thought I had a good sense of the injustice of "justice" and wrote an article in a national magazine about it. Like many advocates for defendants, though, I didn't know much about crime victims, and I wasn't motivated to learn. I also was deeply skeptical of anyone working in "the system."

In 1978 I moved to Elkhart, Indiana, where I had lived when starting college. I took some graduate classes while directing a half-way house for formerly incarcerated men, but it soon burned down. I was then asked to get involved in the new idea of bringing victims and offenders together. I was deeply skeptical, but when I got involved and saw what happened in these encounters, my whole lens on justice changed.

An early case in my work in Indiana sticks in my mind. Two young men had burglarized a home and were referred to our program. Accompanied by a trained facilitator, they met with the couple they had burglarized, in their home.

As restitution, the couple asked the young men to buy a piece of furniture that fit the décor of their home, for two reasons: they wanted the young men to learn to know them well enough to buy the right thing, and they wanted to be able to tell their friends that their burglars bought it for them. The young men and the couple ended up shopping for the furniture together.

Later, the woman ran into one of the young men on the street and, learning that he was heading to a business to apply for a job, said that she knew the owner and would put in a word for him. Something important was happening here, I realized.

BP: Are you saying that your encounter with the "restorative spirit" was a whole journey of encounters with the reality of injustice?

HZ: Absolutely. A circuitous journey with many encounters, many unknowns, and no grand plans. I won't bore you with many of them, but my studies were part of this.

My undergraduate degree was in European history. When I graduated, I had no idea what I wanted to do, but I received several generous fellowships to pursue the area in graduate school. Along the way, I decided I wanted to learn to use quantitative methods and came across some 19th century German crime statistics in the basement of the University of Chicago library. That led to my dissertation research, which involved a statistical analysis of the history of crime in Germany and France in the 19th and early 20th centuries.

I spent 14 months in France and Germany digging statistical records out of archives. An archivist in Berman spent a very long time explaining to me how I would never get a dissertation out of the direction I was pursuing. The dissertation was published in the mid-1970s as *Crime and the Development of Modern Society*, one of the early efforts to use quantitative methods in history.

Interesting, after all these years, it is now being reissued by Routledge Press. That research got me into crime.

It was during this time that I also got into photography, in another circuitous way! When I visited archives, I needed to record statistical documents for later analysis. Many small archives didn't have copiers in 1969-70, so I rigged up a camera on a tripod, with a lighting system made from tin vegetable cans, and made my own microfilm.

Then I got hooked on the camera as a way of seeing and exploring the world. Eventually I found ways to combine my justice and photography passions.

I never imagined the way my different lines of study and my various experiences would come together to prepare me for the future. For example, history was the perfect preparation. It emphasized the crafts of writing and of synthesis. I've come to understand that the concept of Restorative Justice is a work of synthesis rather than invention. I pulled together different ideas and practices, including my own "indigenous" and religious traditions, into what I hoped was a coherent concept that communicated well to others.

During my graduate studies, the history of science was one of my fields. That introduced me to the idea of paradigms, which turned out to be important for my proposals about the "lenses" we use for justice.

Based on my experience, I've often advised my students not to worry too much about what direction their futures will take, but rather to pursue their passions and to be open to signs and opportunities along the way. And I've often told them not to take grades too seriously. At Morehouse College, it was said that when he was a student, Dr. Martin Luther King, Jr.—one of the greatest orators in history—once got a C in speech.

BP: You embody without doubt great rigor in your being, despite the modesty you transmit—and most importantly, *choose* to transmit—because without rigor none of the wonderful and many things you have done would have been possible. But also, an attitude that comes across here is your attitude of openness, or what you call wonder. Wonder is what children have the very first time they do things. How did you preserve wonder within yourself?

HZ: So much of our education in the West, as well as many of our faith traditions, emphasize that we have to *know* things, to *be sure* of things. But an attitude of humility reminds us that we don't have to—can't—and that there are wonderful surprises in not knowing sometimes.

I taught a class called Contemplative Photography. Approached in the right attitude, the camera—and the arts in general—can help us stay connected with the sense of wonder.

BP: You have transposed the metaphor of photography into Restorative Justice and vice versa. Many of your books—I am thinking of *Doing Life: Reflections Of Men And Women Serving Life Sentences,* of *Transcending: Reflections Of Crime Victims,* and of *What Will Happen To Me?*—bring together a type of photography and narration which is simple but not simplifying.

There is something very appealing in your photographs because they "tell it like it is." People are themselves in the most human and intimate way, not beautified, not made to feel sympathy with, but made to be encountered. There is a sense of possibility and a hope. People seem to transcend what they are, where they are, what they have done, or what has been done to them. Don't they all in a way seem to say that life is a movement, and comes with the wrongs we do to each other, and harms that are done to us? But that this, in a way, is our life material, the stuff we are made of?

HZ: My goal in *Doing Life* and in others, such as *Transcending,* has been to humanize those I interview and photograph, so that we see and listen to them without our stereotypes getting in the way.

With the lifers, I deliberately left out those indicators that trigger our stereotypes such as bars and tattoos. I portray them as I would want to be portrayed. All of us are more than the worst things we have done or have experienced.

Before I did the book, the lifer project was a photo exhibit with excerpted interviews from each person. It was shown at a conference held at one of the prisons where many of the men were held. The assistant warden approached me about the exhibit. I expected him to say that I was being naïve, or that I didn't know the whole story. Instead, he said, "I'm glad you did this. You get them just right."

BP: I am curious about another book of yours that no one in the Restorative Justice field seems to know about— *Pickups, A love story*. What does Howard Zehr have to do with truck drivers?!

HZ: Pickup trucks are a big thing in America. Years ago my publishers Merle Good and Phyllis Pellman Good suggested a book about this, but I wasn't ready to do it. But after three photo/interview books with tough, traumatic topics, I was ready for a change. It was great fun to get these stories and learn to know the people in the *Pickups* book. I tried to treat everyone with the kind of respect that I did in the other books and to let them speak for themselves.

BP: Yes, it is clear to me that there is a thread throughout your work and your practice, whether you're doing justice, teaching, photography, or pickup stories. From my experience, I will say that it is a blessing for everyone that you express yourself through photography, and that your books are printed, because your handwriting is completely illegible!

But if I may go back to Morehouse College, how did it feel to be the only White boy in an all-Black college, and in what ways was that a formative experience for you? You also mention the influence of Martin Luther King, but I am sure there are also other Black thinkers in your formation.

HZ: Early September 1963 was less than a decade after the U.S. Supreme Court decision, Brown v. Board of Education, desegregating public schools. It was right after the March on Washington. It was also a few weeks before the 16th Street Baptist Church in Birmingham, Alabama, would be bombed and four Black girls would die, though of course no one except the Ku Klux Klan perpetrators knew that yet.

Early that month, at age 19, I left my largely White community in northern Indiana and entered my sophomore year at Morehouse College in Atlanta. Morehouse is an elite, historically Black men's college that has graduated many African American leaders, including Dr. Martin Luther King, Jr. As I said before, he was still listed as faculty there, and I had the privilege of meeting him once.

I had prepared for that year the best I knew how by reading mostly African American writers, especially James Baldwin, Richard Wright, and W.E.B. Dubois, and through talking with people such as Dr. Vincent Harding. An adviser to Dr. King, Dr. Harding had visited our home on several occasions, and I remember sitting at the dining room table with him as he tried to help a naïve, White, high school student understand something about race and justice. Those conversations are part of what prompted me to take this step.

At Morehouse, a number of my professors were important to me, especially my history prof, Dr. Melvin Kennedy. And Morehouse president Benjamin Mays—a mentor to Dr. King—was a model for me. In fact, it was thanks to him that I received a full scholarship for my senior year at Morehouse as a "minority" student.

But nothing could fully prepare me for the cultural, personal, and identity challenges I would face. And really, nothing but an immersion into an environment where I was a distinct minority could teach me the lessons I needed to learn about myself, my assumptions, and the world of my Morehouse brothers. They are lessons that continued to shape my life and work long after I graduated from Morehouse in 1966 as the first White guy. Without them I never would have wandered into this work that we call Restorative Justice.

One invaluable lesson from that experience was the importance of being willing to step into the unknown. I certainly did that in 1963, and when I graduated in 1966 I could never have imagined that the foggy road ahead would lead me into what we now know as Restorative

Justice. Steps into the unknown have led to some of my most important involvements and lessons.

For example, soon after I came to Eastern Mennonite University, I received a call from the attorneys defending Timothy McVeigh, the "Oklahoma City bomber," asking for help so that their work would be more sensitive to victims. Some of my Restorative Justice colleagues warned against such an unpopular and dangerous involvement. I'm happy to say, though, that in spite of the dangers, then EMU president Joe Lapp said, "Go for it!" I answered the call, along with Tammy Krause who was then my student. Out of that came—thanks to Tammy, who is considered the pioneer and leader of that field—an area of work that some say is transforming death penalty legal defense, making it much more receptive to the needs and choices of victims—that is, surviving families and loved ones. So that's one bit of wisdom I'd offer: be willing to step into the unknown.

Another important lesson I learned through my Morehouse experience has to do with the way I see the world. Much of what I think I know, my worldview, in other words, is shaped by who I am and what I have experienced. I am an educated (some might say overeducated) middle-class, White male, a European-American Mennonite, a preacher's kid, an American with certain experiences in my past. All of that shapes how I see the world and what I think I know. Other people have different worldviews, shaped by where they grew up, their cultural frameworks, what they have experienced.

It is essential to remember this when we engage with others. And interactions with those we think of as "other" are crucial today, in this era. So much of our attention is focused on highlighting our differences, often in a negative way. It is by "othering" that we create enemies, whether domestic or international, whether so-called offenders or newcomers to our country, and justify doing bad things to them.

I believe that we need to be humble about what we think we know. This involves a recognition of the limits of what we "know," and an acknowledgment that our perspectives, our "truths," are affected by who we are and what we have experienced. Consequently, it is essential that we engage with those who are different from us, and in an attitude of openness and receptivity. This is especially important in the current polarized environment.

BP: You started doing Restorative Justice around the year I was born, and I am interested, as a member of another generation, in the transmission of ideas between generations. You say that Restorative Justice is a work of synthesis and not a work of invention. You make huge efforts to transmit the passion for this field. You try in your work to make Restorative Justice digestible, communicable, to make it come across, to transmit it to new generations.

Sometimes to do that you have used metaphors. Other times you have used art as a medium. Sometimes you try to strip it down to principles, questions, and definitions. But Restorative Justice is a complex synthesis, and to strip it down is like putting the ocean into bottles. How do you transmit Restorative Justice to new generations without simplifying it too much? And without giving those who come after you the illusion that they can learn it without discovering it by living it themselves and finding their own way?

HZ: I always emphasize that justice is a matter of the heart as well as the head. I have tried to teach in an elective, participatory way. Our pedagogy in our program is based on the idea that, as one of our board members once said, "The education that matters is education that helps learners conceptualize their own experiences."

My self-concept has been as a "learning facilitator," with the goal of creating situations where we draw from everyone's wisdom. I'm happy to say that many of our graduates are now leading the way as a new generation of restorative advocates and practitioners.

BP: Thank you for using your ability to synthesize your "10 Ways to Live Restoratively," (See Chapter 13.) I admit that the one that makes me happiest is number 10: "Sensitively confront everyday injustices." These strike me as amazing life lessons, which are not just principles one decides theoretically, but which call on all of one's life and history.

But one more question: How does it feel to be called the "father" of Restorative Justice? I have heard also "grandfather," which I assume is an effort to acknowledge you even better. Does this please you? Does it put a burden on your shoulders? Do you find it to be a misinterpretation? How do you relate to it?

HZ: I've been called various things, including the "Elvis Presley of Restorative Justice!" But I prefer not to be called the "father." Restorative Justice has many sources and many people involved. I didn't invent it, and it is important to recognize that it has been articulated by women and men from many traditions and perspectives.

●　●　●　●　●　●　●　●　●　●　●

When I left my position as director of the Office on Crime and Justice with Mennonite Central Committee US in 1996 to teach at EMU, I considered that I had probably done what I could within the field of Restorative Justice.

Was I ever wrong! EMU provided a base for so many new involvements. More importantly, it gave me an opportunity to teach, mentor—and learn from—"students" from all over the world. This greatly expanded my understanding of Restorative Justice and its possibilities, and especially as these learners went on to apply Restorative Justice in ways that I had never imagined.

There were so many wonderful surprises. A Pakistani frontier police commander, for his practicum, worked in a maximum security prison for youth and got youth from conflicting gangs—and later even staff—to sit in a circle and talk.

A student from Muslim Tunisia, for his practicum, worked with a Jewish prosecutor, helping a Catholic diocese address clergy sexual abuse.

Ali Gohar from Pakistan, pictured on page 102, realized that the jirga *process in his tradition in Pakistan was a circle process and used Restorative Justice as a way to empower elders to address wrongs and to open the process to women.*

The list could go on and on.

I also learned a great deal about how to teach or, as I prefer to frame it, facilitate learning. Class participants who were involved in theater helped me learn to use drama as a learning strategy. Visual artists and musicians increased my understanding of the use of arts in the classroom. In

When I was interviewing and photographing for the pickup truck book, I was driving a Jeep. That was not considered cool by some pickup lovers. After I bought the truck in this photo I fit in much better.

graduate school my main teaching models were lectures, so this was initially a stretch.

. . . .

In addition to Restorative Justice, when I arrived at CJP I was tasked with teaching the required research course. This turned out to be a favorite course for both the students and me. It was exciting to see participants design and carry out practical, interview-based projects that often included a visual component. Some of these have had long-range consequences.

Eventually the research course was taught by others, but at the end of my teaching career, I was privileged to co-teach a course with Paulette Moore. Entitled "Research as Art and Transformation," it drew on the relatively new field of art-based research.

With CJP graduate Ali Gohar. Ali, a social worker from Pakistan, was much inspired by Restorative Justice and circle processes and has been working actively to connect these with his own tradition in practical ways.

CHAPTER 7

Restorative Justice and the Gandhian Tradition

The following were my remarks when presented with the Mahatma Gandhi Community Service Award by the Mahatma Gandhi Center for Global Nonviolence, James Madison University, in 2013. Sadly, professor Terry Beitzel, director of the Center, who nominated me, died recently as a result of COVID. I appreciate my restorative lawyer friend sujatha baliga's (she prefers to have her name uncapitalized) help with the Gandhian terms below.

As a Mennonite, I grew up in a family and tradition of nonviolence and peacemaking and knew something of Gandhi. But it was at Morehouse College, the historically African American college, from which I graduated in 1966 during the Civil Rights Movement, that I engaged more deeply. So my understanding of the Gandhian tradition was mediated through the work of Dr. Martin Luther King, Jr., Dr. Vincent Harding, my professors, and the Civil Rights activists with whom I came in contact.

After finishing graduate school, I went on to teach at Talladega College, another historically Black college in Alabama, and there became active in criminal justice. All of this is part of the mix that led me into Restorative Justice

Many, and not only those working in the "peacemaking criminology" tradition, have noted that the criminal justice system is based on, and enforced by, violence or the threat of it. Political scientists often note that the essence of the modern state is the "legitimate monopoly of violence," and criminal justice is how this monopoly of violence is enacted and expressed: "You've harmed us, so we'll harm you."

But the Gandhian tradition is otherwise. Three terms are associated with it.

Ahimsa is often translated "nonviolence," but it shouldn't be articulated as a negative. It is a term of positive action grounded in a worldview of respect for one another and a vision of how we live together.

Likewise, Restorative Justice is grounded on the value of respect. Restorative Justice is not just nonviolent but involves a positive act of caring for one another and our needs and our relationships. I often articulate the underlying values of Restorative Justice as the three R's—respect, responsibility, relationships.

In my faith tradition, the vision is expressed in what I call the "shalom triangle": We are called to live in right relationships with each other, the Creator, and the Creation. But regardless of faith tradition, by the nature of the human condition, we are all inevitably embedded in a web of relationships in which our actions affect, and are affected by, others. Both Gandhian and Restorative Justice approaches articulate a vision of respectful relationships in which the dignity and needs of each person are recognized.

Healthy, respectful relationships imply a responsibility for our actions and for each other. This goes beyond passive responsibility, as when we accept a judgment that we have done something wrong. Rather, it calls for what John Braithwaite and others have called "active" responsibility to put things right, an approach to justice as promoting a better future. Thus, the three R's—respect, responsibility, relationship—are intertwined like a triple helix.

Swaraj, the second term, connotes a kind of self-rule. The Gandhian tradition is a movement for self-governance, personally and socially. Similarly, Restorative Justice believes that individuals and communities have the potential and resources to govern themselves. RJ's practices encourage both individuals and communities to call upon their best selves. This is often seen in the power of circle processes that are used widely. Restorative Justice is about developing individuals' and communities' abilities to be self-governing.

Satyayraha, the third term, is often translated as "nonviolent resistance" but more accurately is a "truth force" or action from truth. Again, it is a positive, not a negative. Restorative Justice also represents an active movement toward truth-telling and truth-seeking. While the legal system often discourages a holistic telling of the truth, Restorative Justice encourages it. In fact, Restorative Justice could be—should be—a nonviolent, truth-seeking challenge to the prison-industrial complex that drives our criminal justice system.

I will end with three quotes or paraphrases attributed to Gandhi:

- "An eye for an eye makes the whole world blind." This is a powerful reminder of the dangers of revenge and retribution.
- "Be the change you wish to see." This is often attributed to Gandhi, but it isn't clear whether he said it quite that way.

The closest quote of his I could find is: "If we could change ourselves, the tendencies in the world would also change. As a man changes his own nature, so does the attitude of the world change towards him.... We need not wait to see what others do."

We see this happening in Restorative Justice conferences and circles. Restorative Justice asks us to be this
change—to live it, practice it—as practitioners and also as
participants. Some say we are called to approach Restorative Justice as a way of life.

- "That action alone is just which does not harm either
  party to a dispute." Here is a direct challenge to the
  prevailing criminology of violence.

Again, I thank you for this honor, but let us envision
this award not as an acknowledgment of me personally,
but rather of the many people around the world who are
contributing to the development and spread of Restorative
Justice—a movement that I believe holds much potential
for transforming lives and communities.

* * * * * * * * * *

Again and again I am reminded of the power of respect.
A simple example: At a conference sponsored by a local RJ
program, a young offender and his victims were on stage
to tell their story. The young man had stolen cars from a
local car dealer. Through a meeting with the husband and
wife who owned the business, he had turned his life around
and become friends with them. When we asked him what
it was that made such an impact on him, he kept repeating
that it was the respect he was given by everyone involved.

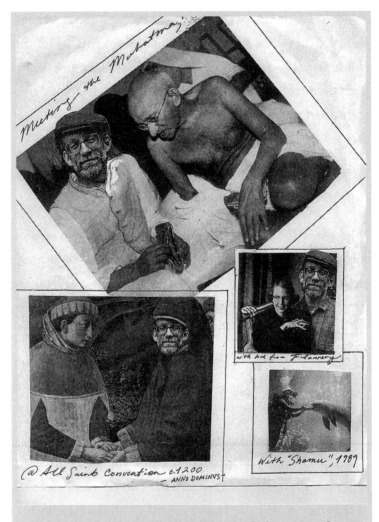

Seeing the photos of my meetings with the pope and Mother Teresa in my office (see Chapter 5), one of my students, Joanna Yoder, put together this spoof collage of me with Gandhi, St. Thomas Aquinas, Flannery O'Connor, and Shamu the dolphin.

. . . .

It means a lot to me when people whom I have photographed tell me that the respectful portrait I have made has caused them to see themselves in a new light. Lifer Raymond Crawford once told me that he and some of the other men I had photographed were thinking of collecting testimonials about this for me. Unfortunately, Raymond died of diabetes before it could happen.

In 1990, I worked with the residents' council of the St. Thomas housing area in New Orleans on a photo/interview project called "The Dreams and Fears of St. Thomas." St. Thomas was widely viewed throughout the city as a symbol of poverty and violence, but there was much more to the community than that. The traveling exhibit that resulted was shown in St. Thomas and then throughout the city. Some in St. Thomas credited this respectful vision of themselves as helping to empower them to undertake a process of transformation in the community. I was asked to return in 1995 and revisit some of the same people, making new photos and doing new interviews. The mood was much more upbeat than it had been five years earlier.

St. Thomas was on prime land in New Orleans, and unfortunately the city eventually managed to tear most of it down for other uses. In 2000, at the request of the St. Thomas leadership, I returned to document the destruction of their community.

CHAPTER 8

Looking Back on My Career and the Field:

Reflections upon receiving an award

I *was asked to give a short talk when I received the Life-time Achievement Award from the* Journal of Law and Religion *at a gathering hosted by Hamline University, St. Paul, Minnesota, in 2006. Hamline was one of the first law schools to incorporate Restorative Justice into its curriculum, so I was pleased to receive the award there.*

About halfway through the Restorative Justice class that I teach, I require my graduate students at the Center for Justice and Peacebuilding to try to explain Restorative Justice to someone who knows nothing about it. The results are often very interesting and sometimes amusing.

One of these participants was Muslim, from Rwanda, and had lost his family in the genocide. He had recently married a Rwandan woman, a Catholic, and he decided to do his assignment with her. He had barely launched into his presentation when she began to laugh: "You came all the way here, spent all this money, just to learn what every African already knows?"

People sometimes comment that they had many of the ideas that Restorative Justice incorporates but had never put them all together. This is certainly true for people from many indigenous or traditional systems, but it also true for most of us who are not from traditional backgrounds.

On my first visit to New Zealand, in 1994, their restorative youth justice system was only five years old. I was taken throughout the islands for interviews on radio, on TV, in community settings. At the end of the visit the chief youth judge, who was Maori, told me, "You don't know how good it is to hear you articulating all this in a way that Westerners can understand. People want to write our system off as Maori." In part, I think Restorative Justice is a way to articulate the best of many of our traditions, but in a way that connects with contemporary Western thought.

In my view, Restorative Justice profoundly resonates with biblical justice. Paradoxically, though, one of the biggest challenges has been to get Christians to rethink their assumptions about punishment and to recognize the restorative themes in their tradition. Restorative Justice does indeed have significant theological implications for Christians.

The metaphor that has guided me in most of my work life has been that of a "journalist of justice." As I got into Restorative Justice work, I set out to be an interpreter, to conceptualize and communicate what was going on. Whatever theory or conceptual framework I have contributed was motivated by a desire to communicate what we were doing and why. And I've been tinkering with that ever since. I see myself basically as a "Volkswagen bug" thinker. Over the past 30 years I've been adding bigger tail lights and changing the window size, but working with the same basic frame.

All of this is not a path that I consciously chose. My academic background was in European history, of all things, but then many paths began to converge: my commitment to communication and popular education, my history of science background (that contributed paradigm theory), my history training, my dissertation research in historical crime, my advocacy for prisoners and defendants in the 1970s, my faith, even my photography. Looking back, it is as if all this was a setup.

But it took an "act of God," a fire (talk about a biblical image!), to open my eyes and set me on the path of Restorative Justice. It was when the halfway house I was directing burned, that I (reluctantly, I must admit) got involved in bringing victims and offenders together, and that was my conversion experience. It was then that I began to truly understand what was wrong with justice as we commonly know it and to realize there was another way.

Over the past three decades, the field of Restorative Justice has expanded beyond my wildest imagination. As I look at these developments, my enthusiasm for them is in tension with my concern about the possible—indeed, inevitable—distortions and misuses of the concept. I always tell my students that all interventions have unintended consequences. All will go astray, regardless of our good intentions. Thus, it is essential to hold in tension idealism and realism. In fact, I am much more concerned about the true believer than the skeptic.

Our critics point out that we tend to be like butterfly collectors, focusing on the best specimens. But we also must learn from our mistakes. As one of my former students, Craig Spaulding, has put it, we need to tell both butterfly and bullfrog stories. This isn't easy to do.

Some years ago I was in a workshop where we went around the circle telling stories. Each person had a beautiful story of hope and reconciliation to tell. When it was my turn, I told of a disastrous circle in which we did everything wrong. To use a phrase stolen from someone else, my story went over like a skunk at a garden party. The group went back to their butterfly stories.

One of the many debates in the field is whether Restorative Justice is or should be *transformative* justice. Some say these are two different approaches. Some say they are the same, just using different names. Some say that Restorative Justice is a way station on the road to transformative justice. All three of these positions are true in some sense. My hope is that Restorative Justice will ultimately lead to the transformation of not only individuals, but society as well.

For example, it gives me hope when I hear people talk about "restorative marriage." I know something is happening when a police commander in a Restorative Justice training in Northern Ireland comes in the next day and tells me that when his daughter wrecked the car the night before, he dealt with her much differently than he normally would have—because of Restorative Justice.

I am trying to proactively embrace old-geezerdom. At this point, I believe my primary responsibility is to pass the baton to others. And I'm in a wonderful place to do that. With "students" (my former colleague John Paul Lederach called them "colleagues masquerading as students") who are practitioners from all over the world, my job, as someone has said, is to "create a space where wisdom can come forth." Much wisdom does come forth, and these people go on to take Restorative Justice into arenas and applications that I never could have imagined.

When former student Tammy Krause takes Restorative Justice into the unlikely arena of death penalty litigation, I see the baton pass. When Barb Toews works with prisoners to develop Restorative Justice from their perspective, the baton passes. When former students apply Restorative Justice to help address justice issues in inter-community conflicts in Ghana, the baton has passed.

Through all this, I seek to find balance and personal space in my life, and to encourage my students to do so— to be half-hearted fanatics. I take seriously the admonition of naturalist Edward Abbey who offered a version of this: "Do not burn yourself out. Be as I am. A reluctant enthusiast and a part-time crusader. A half-hearted fanatic. Save the other half of yourselves for pleasure and adventure. It is not enough to fight for the West. It is even more important to enjoy it, while you can, while it's still there." He goes on to say that if you do, he promises that we'll outlive the so-and-sos.

I have sometimes been called a "guru" and an icon of Restorative Justice. I acknowledge that I have some gifts, but others have contributed greatly to this movement. If I'm honest, I recognize that the attention I receive is far beyond what I actually deserve. I recognize that icons and symbols play an important function in a movement. But I'm also aware that this status is more easily conferred on people who are visible through their writing and speaking.

I know that it is more likely that gray-haired White guys are placed in this role than women and people of color. And I know that we usually expect too much of those we put on a pedestal.

But with these caveats, I am deeply honored to receive this award!

• • • • • • • • • • •

The heavy bronze sculpture, by artist Michael B. Price, was designed for the award as an expression of the relationship between law and culture. According to the description accompanying it, the award "... is inspired by the giving of the law at Sinai, though not a representation of it. . . . The people are gathered in relation to each other, around the law. . . .Most important in this image is that the law allows us to have access to ourselves, to each other and to the source of our ethical principles."

I have received several other wonderful sculptures in conjunction with awards. In 2003 the Annual Peacebuilder Award I received from the New York Dispute Resolution Association is a lovely glass sculpture of the Iroquois Tree of Peace by a local artist. The Tree of Peace is where the five warring Native American nations are said to have come together in peace to form a union. According to Wikipeda, a bundle of five needles from the tree became a symbol of the nations living together as one.

At a training for the Thames Valley Police (U.K.) I was made an honorary constable. A questionable "award," perhaps, but the publishers thought it too humorous to leave out.

Many people, myself included, are blessed to have learned from, been mentored by, and/or worked directly with Howard Zehr.

Within these pages, readers everywhere can benefit from Howard's lifetime of experiences, living and teaching Restorative Justice.

Thank you, Howard.

—*Thomas Norman DeWolf, author and co-manager of Coming to the Table*

I remember when I was working at James Madison University (JMU), my supervisor said, "You have to take a Restorative Justice course from Howard Zehr at Eastern Mennonite University across town. People come from all over the world to learn from him."

I had never heard of Howard Zehr or Restorative Justice at the time, but if JMU was willing to pay, I'd try it. It turned out to be one of the best experiences of my life, and I met a teacher, a role model, a mentor, and a wonderful friend.

From the very beginning, Howard made an impression on me. For a man who was so well known, he was so humble, unassuming, and, more than anything else, lived restoratively.

I learned more about Restorative Justice just watching Howard and how he carried himself than from all the books I would read on the subject. For a man so famous, he always took the time to help me, push me forward, and connect me with people who could help my career. If it wasn't for Howard I never would have connected to Restorative Justice and been able to implement Restorative Justice practices at JMU.

When years later I was thinking of writing a book on Restorative Justice, Howard was there—supporting me, encouraging me, and writing an amazing endorsement. Howard has inspired me to live a life dedicated to justice and peace, just like him.

—*Josh Bacon, author of* I Screwed Up! Now What? *and former dean of students, James Madison University*

Since I met Howard 30 years ago, he has been my mentor, professor, collaborator, and friend. I have experienced first-hand his many traits that shine through in this book and take them as lessons on how to be in this world — practice humility, reflect critically, honor and seek out others' contributions, and embrace humor. Howard generously shares of his personal life, offering a glimpse into his hobbies, friendships, and family. It is the lessons from when Howard is not being the "grandfather of Restorative Justice" that stand out to me: embrace your inner geek, savor a good cup of coffee, and return emails promptly.

—*Barb Toews, RJ educator and practitioner, University of Washington Tacoma*

Howard has continuously given impressive messages to my Restorative Justice class students at Waseda Law School for many years. He has greatly influenced Japanese lawyers with a restorative mind.

—*Kei Someda, Faculty of Law, Surugadai University, Saitama, Japan*

I am excited for this book's publication!

This collection of Dr. Zehr's writing and art reflects so much of what I admire about him—his deep humility, gentle and generous spirit, abiding capacity for awe and wonder, accessible communication style, and ever-deepening reflection on the profound sources that have shaped his thinking—such as his Anabaptist Christian faith and his education at Morehouse.

This book may be the next best thing to sitting in the audience of the lectures Howard delivered in classrooms for my students. Or being on the other end of the phone listening to his amazing—and often hilarious!—stories.

—*Johonna McCants-Turner, Ph.D., associate professor of Peace and Conflict Studies, Conrad Grebel University College, and former co-director, Zehr Institute for Restorative Justice*

I became a volunteer "mediator" for the program under Howard's tutelage and, after witnessing the outcomes in one of my first cases, I was hooked. The referral Howard had assigned me involved two co-accused "offenders" responsible for many hundreds of dollars of losses for the "victim" (the owner of a car dealership who ultimately hired the youth to enable them to pay their restitution to him, then continued to employ them part-time while they finished high school).

Little did I know that that experience would begin to define a good deal of the rest of my professional life. Profound thanks, Howard!

—David Gustafson, researcher and developer of (the now national) Victim Offender Mediation Program (aka Restorative Opportunities) in Canada's prison system

Howard's rooted humility, consistent integrity to life-giving values, and commitment to reflective practice have significantly contributed to a foundation from which to walk my personal, family, and work life journey.

—Matthew Hartman, Just Outcomes

I often use one word when I describe Howard to people—humility. A word I don't use freely or often, but it describes him.

For Howard, the word humility means having an understanding of what you don't know and listening to the wisdom of others. And, he, more than anyone I know has lived that out.

I remember as we started talking about the values of Restorative Justice being something we also needed to practice in our own lives...and are still figuring out and practicing...that he would sometimes say to me, "If I haven't told you lately, I really do appreciate working with you."

That's Howard.

—Lorraine Stutzman Amstutz, Restorative Justice leader and author

How wonderful that this book multiplies the blessing of Howard's insights, stories, and spirit.

A number of years ago, Howard invited me to co-write the preface for a new book. Through this collaboration, I bore witness to Howard's generous leadership, discerning attention, and boundless web of relationships.

In sharing from his own Christian peacemaking roots, Howard helped me (and countless others) to recognize the power and responsibility of reclaiming my own.

—*Caitlin Morneau, Director of Restorative Justice, Catholic Mobilization Network, Washington, D.C.*

Changing Lenses, Howard Zehr's seminal work, is a revelation.

The idea that we are witnessing a paradigm shift from a justice that reproduces harm to one that heals harm was — and still is — startling, welcome and generative.

Today, the need to re-imagine justice is ever more urgent. Indeed, in the aftermath of the public lynching of George Floyd, we live in a time of reimagining new justice futures.

—*Fania E. Davis, Ph.D. in Indigenous Knowledge, leading national voice on Restorative Justice, Civil Rights trial attorney, educator*

Howard Zehr is a visionary.

I believe this not because of his many impressive teachings and writings. I say this because of how Howard demonstrates these teachings through his life. Those who have met Howard know that, through his humility and humanity, he makes you feel special. Nowadays, it is hard to find true visionaries, or indeed get inspired. I am grateful I got to meet Howard during the early stages of my career and see through his lenses, feel special, and get inspired. I have now learned to observe my own reality and through this view find the strength to rise to the challenge that he is leaving us with.

—*Theo Gavrielides, legal philosopher and Restorative Justice expert, London, England*

My friendship with Howard formed over art and photography. He helped me design and set up my first darkroom and talked me into buying a couple of *very* sketchy Russian-made cameras. He's accompanied me on projects, and we've done plenty of catch-and-release photography together.

After photographing, sometimes, we share an espresso right there in the field that he's made using his customized portable espresso kit and served with an Andes mint.

Everything Howard tells us about himself in this book comes together in those small steaming cups: an expression of communion shared over the hood of a pickup.

—*Scott Jost, professor of art, Bridgewater College*

Howard has shown to many, worldwide, how we can fundamentally re-think our understandings of crime and justice.

He has done so by linking practice to theory, by confronting social systems to the daily world life of people.

—*Ivo Aertsen, editor of the* International Journal of Restorative Justice, *University of Leuven, Belgium*

Howard Zehr has made a huge difference in my life and that of the Mural Arts Program. His writings introduced us to the world of Restorative Justice, and his kindness, empathy, support, and deep belief in the power of the art helped to advance our work in prisons and with those coming home.

He validated our belief that all people have a right to be heard, to be seen and respected; that people need to leave traces of themselves and the meanings they generate in their lives. They need to give expression to all that has happened to them, to say "We are here," and to create beauty.

I am grateful to Howard for underscoring the importance of recovering meaning and finding justice through art.

—*Jane Golden, executive director, Mural Arts Philadelphia*

PART 3

Photography, Art—and Radio—at the Healing Edge

CHAPTER 9

The Meaning of Life: Working at the Healing Edge

*first gave this essay as a keynote address in 1998 at the Summer Peacebuilding Institute at Eastern Mennonite University. My book **Doing Life: Reflections of Men and Women Serving Life Sentences** had been released two years earlier. I very much wanted to use a similar approach with victims of crime but was struggling to conceive the project in a way that did justice to them. Eventually, and in conversation with victims and victim advocates, I did undertake such a project. **Transcending: Reflections of Crime Victims** is the result. Although it is not mentioned in this essay, I believe the values and principles I outline here were essential to it as well.*

*In 2017, I received permission to return to re-interview and photograph some of the lifers from **Doing Life**. It was wonderful to be reunited with them. These are presented in a new book, **Still Doing Life: 22 Lifers, 25 Years Later**, published by The New Press (2022) and co-authored with Barb Toews.*

Gaye Morley, early 1990s and 2017. From *Still Doing Life.*

Two themes have been important in my life—doing documentary work and Restorative Justice. They represent a kind of tension, and I sometimes feel like my head is being split into two parts.

On the one hand, I am a photographer. I have spent almost 15 years of my life earning some of my income as a part-time photographer. I've done landscapes and ads. I've photographed dead fish in a briefcase on a beach and goldfish in a bubblegum machine. I've done photojournalism in more than 20 countries. But what I like doing most is documentary work, using photography to explore and communicate people's realities to other people who do not know them.

I also enjoy interviewing and using photographs combined with words. I find photographs by themselves to be rather ambiguous. I see interviews as a way to help people share themselves, a way to begin to bridge the chasms that separate people. I once read a quote from an artist who said, "Artists are supposed to be on the cutting edge. I want to be at the healing edge." My vision is to use photography as a way to be on the healing edge.

The other part of my career has been in criminal justice, encouraging people to rethink what they think they know about crime and justice. Again, my aim is to be on the healing edge rather than the cutting edge.

More than anything else I had undertaken earlier, a documentary project I did with people serving life sentences, *Doing Life,* brought together the two sides of my life, and it has been very satisfying.

It has been satisfying when lifers tell me that the experience of being interviewed and viewing themselves in photographs has transformed the way they see themselves. It is rewarding when people tell me they are using this book with young people in detention, to help them reflect on their lives. It was especially rewarding to receive a letter from a crime victim who said, "I can't believe I am writing this letter, but I would like to be in contact with some of the people in your book who are offenders."

The project has also been a source of discomfort because it presents only one side of a complicated equation, the "offender's" side. Still, for me personally, it has been an effort to bring together that split in my life.

Four major themes came together in the *Doing Life* project for me. One is the idea of relational social distance. The social distance we feel from other people affects how we perceive and treat "them," and what we expect of "them." With relational social distance we can turn other people into objects, and then we can do all kinds of awful things to "them." They become the "other." In her eloquent essay in *The Handbook of Qualitative Research* (1st ed.), researcher Michelle Fine notes that much—maybe most—research, as well as journalism, has been "a colonizing discourse of the other." The same is true of photography.

Relational social distance is what makes it possible to punish so many people in this country. Nearly six and a half million people are under the control of the criminal justice system on any given day in America. As Norwegian criminologist Nils Christie has pointed out, you can't punish people in this way when you know them well, when you know them in all their complexities and nuances as real human beings.

Relational social distance is also what makes it possible to neglect victims so profoundly. We turn them into abstractions and stereotypes and symbols instead of real people. The modern legal system does this, turning the whole process of justice into a kind of abstract drama in which victims and offenders are stereotypes, and the process itself is mystified.

Interestingly, it's through relational social distance that offenders do what they do as well. They can victimize others because they do not empathize with the victim. Many—perhaps most—offenders commit their offenses by using what psychologists call "neutralizing strategies" such as rationalizations and stereotypes as a way not to think of the victim as a person.

Relational social distance is key. My goal in *Doing Life*, and the goal in Restorative Justice, is to find a way to reduce this social distance.

A second theme that emerged for me with *Doing Life* is what Ezzat Fattah, a victimologist in British Columbia, has called the "transformation of victims into victimizers." We are so preoccupied with punishment that we rarely realize that punishment doesn't work. One study reviewed 23,000 literature references on punishment and could not find any significant evidence that punishment changed people for better.

Most offenders think of themselves as victims. Many have in fact been victims, and their experience of the justice system has caused them to feel victimized as well, simply confirming their self-image. Questions of who was the victim and what is owed to victims surfaced often in my interviews for *Doing Life*.

A third theme I've bumped up against is about how people construct meaning from very difficult circumstances.

In the lifers' quotes, you see people trying to construct meaning out of the awful things they've done and the things they have experienced since that time.

Pennsylvania lifer Irvin Moore said it like this,

> *"Life" to us has two meanings. Life is life, the generic term. Being alive, waking up every day. Life is also a sentence you serve. In Pennsylvania, life is to be served until you die.*

It was that double meaning I wanted to explore, where people had taken a life and now were serving a life sentence. What had they learned? How had they constructed meaning from the experience? That is also what victims of crime struggle with. I am more and more convinced that justice is about the construction of meaning.

A fourth theme: Albert Renger-Patzsch, a photographer in the early 20th century, said, "Photography seems to me to be better suited for doing justice to an object than for expressing artistic individuality." That's my goal: to do justice to the subject.

I got the idea for this project from a friend serving a life sentence in Alabama. One day he wrote, "A life sentence is like trying to keep a candle lit in a dark tunnel." I began to wonder how men and women serving life sentences envision their situations? What metaphors do they use? How do they understand what they did? In the end, I interviewed and photographed about 70 men and women serving life sentences in Pennsylvania.

I thought a lot about how to present these people. I wanted to present them honestly, but also without the stereotypical clues that most photographers include with people who have offended. So I used a plain backdrop and got permission for them to wear whatever street clothes they were allowed to have. I tried to find a way to work with them collaboratively that gave back. I tried to "do justice" to my subjects.

In the area of crime, that question also intrigues me. What does it really mean to do justice? In the Hebrew and Christian scriptures, the prophet Micah begins his answer to the question, "What does the Lord require?" by saying, "To do justice." For me the question that follows is central: "What does justice require?"

The legal system assumes that the needs of victims are irrelevant to the process. It assumes that an offender's obligations to the victim or community has nothing to do with this process. It assumes that the community has no role in justice. It assumes that the wounds that were created by the crime or that led to the crime—or that are created by this adversarial process—are irrelevant to justice.

Restorative Justice answers the question quite differently. It says that what victims require must be the starting point of justice. It answers that offenders' needs and offenders' obligations are central to justice. It says that the community has a role in justice.

We have defined accountability in Western society as returning hurt for hurt, pain for pain. But real accountability is having to understand what you have done and then to take some responsibility for it. One assumption of Restorative Justice is that offenders ought to be held accountable for the harm they've done, and that they have an obligation to make things right.

A second RJ assumption is the major principle of engagement. Instead of justice involving an adversarial exchange between the state and the offender, both operating in a self-protective mode, justice ought to engage all three—the victim, the offender, and the community—in a process that seeks a genuine solution. The outcome should be one that makes things right, as much as possible.

A final RJ theme brings together the two parts of my life—the topic of metaphor. I am more and more convinced that metaphors guide us in how we think. They can be even more fundamental than ideas. Whenever we think and talk about things we cannot see or touch, we usually use metaphor. A metaphor is when we compare one thing to another but do not usually say we are doing it.

While a metaphor is powerful and can have positive implications, it is never a complete picture of what it represents. There is always some part that does not match or is left out. The Bible uses many metaphors for God because we cannot see or touch God. With God we have many metaphors because no single metaphor would be an exact match.

Metaphors can also subtly determine our ideas, often without our realizing it. For instance, in the language of discourse that dominates the Western world, some of the predominant metaphors we use are of war. You "win" an argument. You "shoot down" an opponent's ideas. Our fundamental assumptions are those of conflict.

Deborah Tannen, in her book *The Argument Culture,* asserts that we prize contentiousness and aggression in our public discourse more than cooperation and conciliation, and that this "argument culture" rests on the assumption that opposition is the best way to get anything done. To Tannen, the most dangerous part of this epic of aggression and

Metaphors figure prominently in both *Doing Life* and *Transcending*: a whirlpool trying to suck you in (life-sentenced Marilyn Dobrolinski), a ladder without rungs (survivor Lynn Shiner). Having no other words to describe their extreme experiences, those who have experienced trauma rely heavily on metaphor to express their experiences.

As one therapist told me, my job when helping someone who has experienced trauma is to help them identify the metaphor of trauma that is governing their life; then to replace it with a metaphor of hope.

ritual fighting is "an atmosphere of animosity that spreads like a fever." But what if we were to use instead the metaphor of dance? It would take us in quite a different direction.

In the language of photography we "take" or "shoot" a picture, and we put a camera in front of our eye as if it were a weapon. Ads in the photography magazines have a "shoot out" between types of cameras. They sell an "arsenal of lenses." This is the language of the hunt with the photographer as predator. I would like to change that metaphor and see photography become subject-oriented, to be used in a way that empowers people, that collaborates with people, that gives people voice and visibility. I would like us to learn the language of receiving rather than taking.

Think about how a photographic image happens. We cannot reach out and take an image. The light reflects it back to us and we *receive* the image. The metaphor of meditation is much more appropriate than that of the hunt. In *Doing Life* I was trying to put into practice what I believe about photography as receiving.

Similarly, research often uses metaphors that come from the language of the hunt. I believe there is another way to think about research. In my research methods classes, we have begun to develop guidelines and values for what we call "transformative research."

This is a type of research that is less about creating pure knowledge and instead aims at social action, building community, promoting dialogue, reducing relational social distance, challenging comforting myths, empowering individuals and communities to solve problems, giving voice to marginalized people, promoting justice.

Transformative inquiry respects subjects by promoting values such as collaboration, participation, empowerment, accountability, confidentiality, acknowledgment of obligations to the subject, transparency of goals, methods, and motives, benefits to the subject, and opportunity for subjects to present themselves in their own voices.

I am looking for a metaphor and for the model of research and of justice that respects. Increasingly I am convinced that crime is fundamentally about disrespect. Victims experience crime as profound disrespect. What they want from justice is to be respected. But too often that does not happen.

I am also convinced that disrespect is why offenders commit many of the offenses they do. It is an effort to get respect, but in an illegitimate way. If we are going to address this crisis, we are going to have to find a justice that respects. And that, I think, is what the core of Restorative Justice is about. It is meeting the requirements of justice and doing that with respect.

In *Doing Life* I sought to do photography that respects. I also sought to do photography that speaks to the power of connectedness and that calls us into relationship. I hope I have done justice to the subject.

. . . .

Although my documentary and portrait work has probably been my most meaningful photography, my international photojournalism for Mennonite Central Committee offered the most adventures. Some of these were positive: I have fond memories of flying over the Rift Valley in Kenya in a small plane, watching thunderclouds build; of flying over the Kalahari desert as the sun went down, the plane trying to land in the short window before it got dark; flying low over the desert landscape of Southern Sudan in the evening light with the C130 cargo door open so that we could watch the animals below; sitting under a tree in Southern Sudan, talking international politics with a rebel commander; walking with Laotian villagers through rice paddies as I photographed de-mining efforts; sharing meals with villagers in India, Nicaragua, and other places.

But then there are the times best experienced in retrospect. These include nearly being shot down by rebels while in a Russian Antonov plane over South Sudan during the civil war; sleeping in a bombed-out hospital in the middle of nowhere while shadowy figures moved around in the dark; sleeping in grass huts in a rebel leaders' camp when there were rumors of an attack by a rival rebel group.

I believe my first prison photography was at Angola State Penitentiary in Louisiana. The following comes from the photography journal I began some time ago. The close-cropped style seems to foreshadow my photos in Doing Life, *15 years later.*

Death Row, Angola State Penitentiary, LA, 1981

Tim Baldwin was one of the death row inmates I photographed on this visit, arranged by capital defense attorneys. A journalist friend who investigated the case is confident that Tim was innocent of the crime and that his conviction was due to police incompetence or, more likely, misconduct. Tim was executed by electrocution three years after this photo, in 1984. He was 46.

According to internet-based Murderpedia, these were his final words: "I've always tried to be a good sport when I've lost at something, and I see no reason not to leave this world with the same policy. After all, it was a hell of a battle. I therefore congratulate all those who have tried so hard to murder me. I definitely have to give them credit as it takes a very special kind of person to murder an innocent man and still be able to live with themselves."

Several years after Doing Life *was released, one of the survivors whose story is in my book,* Transcending, *contacted me to say, "I can't believe I am asking this, but next time you go to prison, may I go with you?"*

We invited her to attend a new play by theater artist Ingrid DeSanctis when it was scheduled to premiere at Graterford prison. The play was presented in a large auditorium with hundreds of men in attendance, and the superintendent warned us that at the last event, everyone had walked out. But no one did; in fact, the audience was totally silent and attentive.

At the end of the play, Ingrid, the actors, and I were asked to sit on stage to answer questions. Our guest's story was in the play, and someone asked a question about her motivation. Wishing to keep her identity secret, Ingrid began to answer but our guest interrupted, identifying herself and answering that question and others.

Afterward, men crowded around her, asking her questions, expressing their remorse. It was a moving experience. Later she went on to visit prisons, meeting with men and women there to tell her story and interact with them. Art is powerful!

The lifers' association at Graterford prison was an important source of inspiration and guidance for the photo/interview project that eventually became the book *Doing Life*. In 1992 they presented me with an award. Bruce Bainbridge is on the left. On the right is Tyrone Werts, president of the lifers. Tyrone's sentence was eventually commuted, and he was released. Thirty plus years later, I remain in regular touch with Bruce.

The lifer project was an exhibit before it was a book. The exhibit was displayed at a banquet for family members at Graterford prison. Department of Corrections staff member Bessie Williams is on the left and lifer Tyrone Werts on the right.

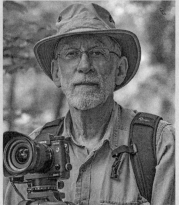

In addition to portraits, I have very much enjoyed landscape photography. Earlier I worked with large format wooden field cameras, and now with digital. A few changes are apparent—and not only in the gear—between the first photo from the late 1980s and the 2019 one! Both of these images were done by my long-time friend and internationally-known ceramic artist, Dick Lehman.

CHAPTER 10

When a Parent Is in Prison

The young girl pictured here is featured in the book,
What Will Happen to Me? which I did with my long-
time colleague Lorraine Stutzman Amstutz. We wanted to
give voice and visibility to the estimated three million chil-
dren who have one or both parents in prison or jail.

Beyond that, we aimed to help those who work with
these children—schoolteachers, social workers, grandpar-
ents who raise them—better understand their experiences
and perspectives. For this project, I was the photographer,
and others, including Lorraine, did the interviewing.

Jasmine is one of three million children in the U.S. who
have one or both parents in prison. They are the hidden victims, the collateral damage, of crime and our prison policies.

These children face the challenges encountered by all
children who are missing parents. But they are confronted
by additional layers of difficulty. They often experience

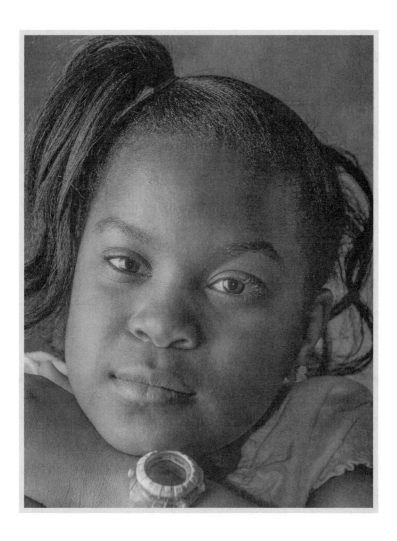

shame and guilt by association; consequently, they feel very isolated.

Sometimes *they* feel guilty—perhaps they have somehow contributed to their parent's situation.

They are anxious about their parents, about their elderly caregivers, about their own well-being and future. They struggle with loss and longing.

Often they are not told the truth about where their parents are or what they have done. This often leads to serious trust issues.

They are frequently angry. In the book, for example, Taylor says she was mad at everyone, at the world. She didn't want to talk to anyone and took her anger out on others.

"You have to grow up fast," many of the older children comment.

As we listened to and photographed these children, we were deeply moved by their struggles, but also their insights and resilience.

A Restorative Justice approach means that those victimized by crime should be much more central to justice than is currently the case. Although first priority should be given to the *direct* victims of crime, others who have been harmed have a stake as well. An overall goal of Restorative Justice is to heal the far-reaching harms of crime. This concern to understand and address the harms of crime led co-author Lorraine Stutzman Amstutz and me to this project.

Some children of prisoners are overwhelmed by their experiences. The trauma will affect them for the rest of their lives and quite possibly will be carried on into future generations. Trauma is often intergenerational. Some of these children's children may end up in prison because of this.

But through struggle and perseverance, some children are able to transcend their trauma. During recent speaking engagements in one of the cities where these interviews took place, I met several of the older children, two years after I had interviewed them. They were doing remarkably well, due in large part to the presence of significant caregivers or mentors in their lives.

In the book, teenager Taylor says, "It really affects us, the kids. It really does. And I want [other kids] to know that we'll get through it. As long as we have somebody that's there to help us, we can get through it. It makes you stronger—I know it's made me stronger."

Stacy Bouchet describes the many issues she struggled with because her father was in prison. She now has her Ph.D. and [at the time of the interview with her] works with an organization that promotes positive fatherhood. She ended her interview saying that the incarceration of a parent should be a signal to communities and systems that there are things going on with families that need to be addressed.

With approximately two million people in prison, many of them parents, something is indeed going on in families.

● ● ● ● ● ● ● ● ● ● ●

One of our CJP graduates, Jenn Dorsch, used this book to spark conversations within her Secret Sisters group at GIRLS, Inc., where she worked. During weekly meetings of these girls who had incarcerated parents, participants read from the book and discussed how it connected with their own lives. One girl's mother said that it had given her daughter "the tools she needs to deal with any big emotional things that come along."

Jenn invited me to participate in a banquet for these girls by setting up a photo studio and doing portraits of the girls and available family members. It was great fun collaborating with them to portray themselves as they wished.

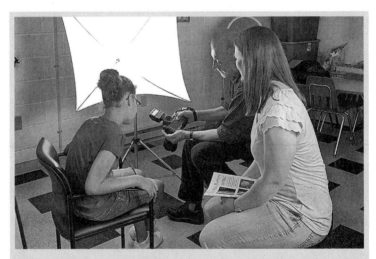

Photographing the Secret Sisters. Here I am showing one of them what we have so far and asking whether she is satisfied and whether she has other ideas for how she wants to present herself.

CHAPTER 11

Amateur Radio for Boys and Geezers

I am an inventor, builder, and tinkerer by nature, and for much of my life, electronics has been a focus of this activity. Building things, finding solutions to problems, and repairing and restoring electronic gear has been a source of energy and balance for me, an outlet for creative energy. A few years ago I explored this a bit in the following previously-unpublished essay.

Sometimes I feel like an anachronism—a septuagenarian amateur radio operator in the internet age, and a ham radio hobbyist who operates almost exclusively with the Morse code, a form of communication not even required for emergency use anymore. But I'm not alone. There is a whole generation of us who got into this as boys in the 1950s and are still at it.

Amateur radio itself may seem an anachronism in the age of cell phones and the internet. Actually, though, there are more licensed operators today than ever before. This is due, in part, to the new platforms and modes available:

satellite communications, moon bounce, a variety of digital modes, new experimental frequencies, new electronic technologies, new frontiers to explore. And while women amateurs remain a distinct minority, their numbers are increasing.

But there is this cadre of old guys—yes, mostly guys—still involved, still doing Morse code, still tinkering, me included.

This was my "shack" (bedroom, actually) when I was maybe 16 or 17. We lived in the parsonage next door to the church where my father was pastor, and my voice would sometimes come over the public address system in the sanctuary. Once I had skipped church and was calling, as I recall, a station whose phonetics were "King George's Donkey." Suddenly my mother came roaring in. Others in church may not have figured out what was happening, but she certainly had!

Lately I've been pondering two questions: Why did so many of us as young boys in the 1950s get into amateur radio? And why, now in our senior years, are we still at it? Is it nostalgia, or is it more than that?

Susan Douglas's interesting and informative book on the history of radio, *Listening In: Radio and the American Imagination,* has some suggestions about the first question. In her chapter on ham radio ("Why Ham Radio Matters"), she proposes that the interest among boys was partly due to what was happening in the '50s generally, and partly due to the nature of twentieth-century masculinity.

This was the post-World War II era. Radio waves were once again free for nonmilitary use. Electronic parts and equipment were becoming readily available and affordable through military surplus and new manufacturing. Radio was, however, in many ways still in its infancy, with much yet to be discovered, often by amateurs. The radio spectrum was, as Douglas says, an undeveloped wilderness, an ethereal extension of the American frontier: democratic, unpredictable, mysterious, open to exploration and discovery. Between 1954 and 1959—the years when I took my test and was licensed—the number of ham operators nearly doubled.

Radio provided a way for boys to pursue elements of masculinity as defined in the mid-20th century, says Douglas, without embracing the more extreme ideas represented by John Wayne or even mainstream culture. It provided a way, perhaps, for boys who didn't quite fit the prevailing expectations of masculinity to find a place.

Boys like me.

I was shy, an introvert. I was not very competitive and not at all interested in sports. Though not diagnosed—we didn't have the terms in those days—I may have been a bit hyperactive, or at least what is now called a kinetic learner, needing to engage my hands as well as my head. I loved to invent and tinker, often fashioning things out of junk parts. Electronics, and especially radio, provided an arena in which I could explore, imagine, create, develop skills, and even achieve some level of technological competence. While most boys were trying to master sports, I was trying to master electronics.

Radio, and electronics generally, also provided a way to connect with others. While trying to figure out why the crystal radio I won on my paper route didn't work, I met local ham operators and an elderly radio repairman in the small town where I lived. I was learning to network—a skill which would turn out to be vocationally important. On the air I chatted with people around the world with similar interests. Even though our conversations were often short and not very profound, there was a connection. Locally, I found a few peers who shared my interests.

Ham radio is and was a subculture with its own rituals, mores, and language, a kind of tribe or fraternity that provides a sense of community and belonging. Today I wonder whether, without this focus, meaning, and community, I might have become a depressed, marginalized kid.

Douglas argues that radio provided young men a way to connect with others with similar interests "on some mystical, metaphorical level" that didn't necessarily mean physical connection. Like sports, but much less aggressively, it allowed for a kind of individualized competence and competition, balanced by a high degree of cooperation and teamwork. Ham radio, she says, is a place where men could "escape the constraints of conventionalized masculinity" while still finding ways to pursue masculine traits and interests. Competition in this arena was self-consciously tempered by what some consider more "feminine" traits of cooperation, altruism, and mutual support. It provided a place to belong.

This explanation probably does not fit everyone who got into radio during this era. But much does ring true, for me at least.

It helps me understand why I, why we, got into this in the first place. But why am I—why are we—still active in this area? Or maybe I should ask, why have I returned to it? Like many men in my cohort, I was off the air (QRT, in radio-ese) during much of my work and family life, reengaging during my 50s after the children were gone, becoming more active as I moved toward retirement.

Involvement in a radio is a way for us retirees to stay engaged and keep our minds active. It is a way of being part of a rather democratic community, a subculture, that spans class barriers. And overall, as I often tell myself, it's cheaper than golf.

I don't have any research—only impressions—so from here on I'll just speak for myself.

I used to fish, using ultralight gear to increase the challenge and excitement. Concerned about the current environmental impact on fish, and becoming more aware that I was hurting a living creature, I have given up fishing. However, radio is a kind of electronic catch-and-release fishing. It relies on skill, involves interesting gear, and has the excitement and serendipity of hooking something or someone you can't see, and no person or creature gets hurt. As in ultralight fishing, some of the time I use low power—"QRP"—to increase the challenge.

Within the subculture of ham radio, there is a whole other subculture of QRP builders and operators, and outside my local geographical area, it is this radio community to which I am most connected. I am part of several online groups dedicated to QRP equipment and a member of several national organizations. In fact, I often write for one of their journals and several years ago was invited to speak at a national seminar. (My topic: "Here we go loopty-loop: magnetic loop antennas for the thrifty QRPer.")

While not true for everyone involved, for me radio is and always has been about the technical and creative aspects as much as the on-air experience. I love to build, restore, customize equipment, to solve technical problems, as much or more than actually being on the air.

As I write this, I'm working with a low-power transceiver, software-controlled, semi-kit designed by a ham operator in India for the explicit purpose of being hacked and improved by the community of hams who work with it. It comes with no warranty and multiple shortcomings. The integrated circuit chip that provides the audio is fragile and probably overdriven; it tends to go up in smoke, as mine did.

Those of us participating in the online community around this radio have shared a variety of work-arounds for this problem. A strong local AM radio station tends to overwhelm the receiver. Based on ideas shared within our group, I found a fix and posted it on line for others. The background noise tends to overwhelm the Morse code signals. I installed an audio filter that fixed that problem. It is now usable, but nowhere nearly as competent as other radios I have. It still presents vexing but intriguing problems to solve. I'll get bored with it if and when it actually works well. [Later note: I eventually did sell it and moved on to other challenges.]

Morse code—"CW," as it is called—is itself a craft and a challenge. When I returned to amateur radio after years away, one of my goals was to become a good CW operator: learning to decode in my head and to send with ideal spacing and rhythm. Good CW is a craft, and when done well, deeply satisfying to send and to "copy" or receive. Often when chatting with someone on the air in the evening, one of us remarks that we are getting in our "CW fix" for the day. I'm always pleased when someone compliments me on my "fist"—that is, my code abilities.

I have been fortunate over the years to have a wide circle of friends, in part through my work in justice and in photography. Unlike some men, I have a number of close male friends. Yet radio continues to provide me with a kind of community of interest that spans vocations and class, a community that becomes more important as I retire from my vocation in justice and education.

This seems true for others as well. Several times a week [this was pre-COVID], a group of ham operators gathers at a local Wendy's for lunch. Most are retired, from a wide range of careers. Attendance varies. I join them from time to time. Sometimes talk is about radio, but often it includes other topics as well—except politics. On the whole, there is a shared understanding in amateur radio that politics is off-limits.

Douglas concludes her chapter like this: "Behind the stereotype of 'old fat guys in basements' are people who insist that radio be participatory, active, noncommercial, educational, personally liberating, and democratic. . . ."

Radio may not give me the physical exercise I need, but it lets me tinker and create and exercise my brain. It keeps me connected. The characteristics listed by Douglas above resonate with my values. And it's cheaper than golf.

In my "shack" (a corner of my office) in early 2022. No microphone in sight—I'm CW (Morse code) only now. The radio on the shelf to my right is an updated model of the radio from India mentioned above. A current project is to improve this version.

• • • • • • • • • • •

I lost contact with one of my best friends at Morehouse College, Jim Richards, after we graduated. A few years ago—50 years later—we found each other. Jim is a retired electronics and software engineer whose career was at one of the biggest computer and software companies in the world. For part of this time, as a "Solutions Architect" he was tasked with solving clients' problems. Although he is not an amateur radio operator, we are in contact with one another almost daily as he designs solar and battery solutions, often for the radio community, and I provide ideas and field-test them. Here is another connection and creative outlet enhanced by my electronics interests.

I had the honor of being best man at Jim and Ophelia's secret wedding in 1966, just before graduation from Morehouse College.

In 1957, *Christian Living* magazine, a Mennonite
publication, ran a front-page story written by my mother
about activities for children. It was illustrated with photos
of our family. Here my father is shown demonstrating
how to use our jigsaw. In reality, though, he was a busy
pastor and not all that mechanical, so my brother Ed
and I were the main users. We also had a primitive
table saw with the same setup of motor and pulleys and
no safety guard. Why we still all have our fingers is a
mystery, but Ed remembers that we were very careful.
I believe I got my first radio license the following year.

Howard has changed the way I cut apples.

I love watching how he carefully, lovingly makes slices that preserve every bit except the stem and the seeds, which, of course, he composts.

What a perfect metaphor for how he views the human experience. Nothing is to be discarded, not one single part of any of us.

That's how I've understood Howard's philosophical contribution to the world, but more importantly, it's how I experience him as a mentor and friend. All of me is unconditionally welcome, even the parts I wish weren't true.

What a blessing that truly is.

—sujatha baliga, attorney and Restorative Justice practitioner (winner of the MacArthur Fellowship)

 CONTINUED ON PAGE 218—

PART 4

Restorative Justice: A Vision to Guide and Sustain Us in All of Life

CHAPTER 12

Beyond Crime:
A Vision to Guide
and Sustain Us

In 2018 I was invited to give keynote addresses to conferences in Trieste and Padua, Italy. The University of Padua, founded in 1222, is the world's oldest surviving university. In light of my interests in the parallels between the 17th century scientific revolution and a possible change in how we view justice, and given the importance of the 17th century scientist Galileo on our modern outlook, it was especially meaningful that a part of the proceedings was held in the lecture hall he used at Padua. The event in Trieste preceded a conference on technology, and I was asked to mention some technological factors relevant to RJ.

The following essay is adapted from those lectures.

On November 4, 1995, at 4:40 in the afternoon, Jackie Millar was shot in the head at close range with an exploding bullet. Two boys broke into the friend's house where she was resting while waiting for him to return from working on his tree farm. They took her car keys, then debated which of their guns they would use to shoot her.

"I died," she told me with quiet conviction, "and then I got resurrected. The Lord told me, 'Maybe you can stop one youth if you tell your story....'"

When I met her she was legally blind, with her right hand paralyzed, and she walked with difficulty and talked slowly. But Jackie was visiting prisons, speaking with young men like those who shot her—including one of the men who did shoot her—doing "hug therapy."

She insisted that Craig, who pulled the trigger, is like one of her sons. Another long-time prisoner recounts how she transformed his life when she told him, "You are a human being, and don't let anyone else tell you differently," then gave him a hug.

Most of us don't experience the call or motivation to improve the world, to serve others, this dramatically. Many of us may, in fact, be uncomfortable with the term "service," but my guess is that most everyone involved in the work of peace and justice has experienced some sort of push or call to make the world a better place.

Jackie's story is one of many included in my photo/interview book, *Transcending: Reflections of Crime Victims.*

In the spring of 2017, 25 years after I did the book, *Doing Life: Reflections of Men and Women Serving Life Sentences*, I received permission to revisit some of those lifers.

Yvonne Cloud

I was struck by how many felt called or motivated to do good, to find meaning by helping others.

Yvonne Cloud is one of them. She was in her 20s when I first met her and had now been in prison for 34 years. She came into the room with a detailed resumé in hand, primed to show me how much she had changed over time. During the intervening years, she has become a peer facilitator in a drug and alcohol program and a certified hospice care worker, among many other involvements in the prison. Recently she also became a Certified Peer Specialist and spends much of her time talking with young, recently incarcerated women. [Certified Peer Specialists are people who have been through experiences such as addiction and are trained to work with peers who have similar problems.]

"Back then I was somewhat shy, still in denial, didn't want nobody to know I had a life sentence, barely wanted to talk about it, but one thing stayed the same. Back then I was determined to do the wrong things. Now I still have the same determination, but to do positive things, and to give back to other people what was so freely given to me, and change their lives for the better.

"I tell people all the time in groups, 'I don't have a clue what's going to happen in the future, but I will not stop being positive, and doing positive things, and helping other people change their lives.' Basically my motto is, unfortunately I took a life. Now what I try to do is help save lives. And help people make a difference in their lives."

Craig Datesman

Craig Datesman had been in 35 years when we reconnected. During those years, through a victim-offender dialogue program—one form of Restorative Justice—he was able to meet with a family member of the man he killed. The experience was transformative for him. "You really have to find meaning in life," he observed. "I realize how important service is, how satisfying it is to be helping other people."

Harry Twiggs

Harry Twigs had 46 years in prison when I revisited him. Like Yvonne, he is a Certified Peer Specialist, and his days are filled with working with other prisoners in that role. "I should have been dead a thousand times," he told me. *"But for some reason, God kept me around."*

"I believe that we are blessed with two lives. The first we live, we make all the mistakes. We commit

crimes, we hurt people. But once we come to, and wake up, and move to our second life, we can draw from the first life and see our mistakes. Not only can you help yourself, you are able to help other people. I've been in two interventions just this morning.

"I look on my being in here like Nelson Mandela and compadres at Robben Island. They came to the conclusion that the solution was within them. So they sat and talked 27 years about how to dismantle apartheid."

Harry sees himself as one of the "architects" of today's culture of street crime, with a calling to address it—inside prison for now, "stopping it one person at a time"—but he dreams of doing it outside, on the streets, if his sentence would be commuted by the governor.

Many other lifers described this sense of call, but so also did many of the survivors of violent crime included in *Transcending.*

Following these two photo/interview books, my colleague Lorraine Stutzman Amstutz and I did a similar book highlighting portraits and quotes from children whose parents were incarcerated. Included in *What Will Happen to Me?* are a number of grandparents who were raising these children. They sacrificed their own plans and dreams for retirement to raise the children. That certainly seems to represent a kind of call to serve.

I often hear this commitment to serve others from those who seek to find peace and justice in their lives and beyond. It is certainly a way to make life and life experiences meaningful, and so very important in today's world.

Needing a vision

But service to others can be exhausting, and it is easy to give up, to burn out. A commitment to make the world better is not enough to keep us going. We need a moral vision to guide and sustain us.

For some, this vision comes from religious faith. For some, it comes through philosophical commitments. For a growing number of people, Restorative Justice serves as the needed moral and cultural vision. As we will see later, this vision can be framed in either secular or religious terms.

As individuals, we need a moral vision, but the issue is larger than us. The world as a whole is facing a kind of social/cultural crisis—some would say a spiritual or moral crisis. We know the problems too well.

We—in the United States at least—are a highly individualistic and materialistic society that emphasizes rights over responsibilities. Ours is a punitive culture that often glorifies violence. Today we are a highly polarized society in which few public figures are modeling integrity, respect, or true dialogue.

Globally, we see tremendous religious and ethnic diversity. This provides for rich possibilities, but also has become politically and socially divisive. The need to belong is a fundamental human need. In threatening and uncertain circumstances, we tend to withdraw into our clans and see others as enemies.

Racism runs deep and wide, taking different forms in various places. It represents, in part, an unhealthy way of finding a sense of belonging and defining social boundaries.

The split between the Haves and the Have-Nots is dramatic and growing, at least in the U.S. The visibility of this divide through the media and the internet results in high degrees of what is sometimes termed "relative deprivation." The awareness of being deprived when compared to others makes for a highly volatile situation, fueling crime, rebellion, even so-called terrorism.

Relative deprivation is one of many factors contributing to feelings of shame and humiliation. James Gilligan and others argue that shame is a—maybe *the*—primary cause of violence, from domestic violence to political terror and hate crimes. According to Gilligan in his book, *Violence: A National Epidemic,* shame is at the heart of what makes structural injustice into structural violence.

Awareness is growing of how widespread trauma is, how trauma contributes to harm and to violence, and how trauma is transmitted to others. As is often said in our program's STAR trainings (Strategies for Trauma Awareness and Resiliency) at Eastern Mennonite University, "Trauma that is not transformed is transferred." Trauma that is not addressed is re-enacted in the lives of those immediately affected, but also in the lives of those around them, including their families and even future generations.

And then, of course, there is our disregard of what we humans are doing to the environment.

Technologically, we live in exciting times, when things are possible that those of us who are older could never have dreamed of. Innovation is constant and promises all sorts of possibilities. I am somewhat of a techie and very much enjoy parts of this.

Cell phones, the internet, and inexpensive electronics are giving access to this technology to many marginalized people, making it possible for them to tell their stories, to connect with others who have similar interests, and to have a direct impact on events.

But many are still left out. The visibility of the Haves increases the alienation, the sense of relative deprivation, and the feelings of shame of the Have-Nots. The anonymity of the internet reduces factors that encourage empathy, making it possible to say and do things that we would not in person.

Manipulative use of media and the internet is negatively affecting politics, contributing to polarization, and undermining democracy.

In short, while contributing to connection for some, these forces are also encouraging disconnection and depersonalization. Powerful forces are discouraging empathy and encouraging "othering," an emphasis on how others are different from us. Violence to others becomes most possible when we "other" people, turning them into our enemies. All of this contributes to unhealthy ways of finding a sense of belonging.

Albert Einstein has famously said, "We can't solve problems by using the same kind of thinking we used when we created them." What is required, I would emphasize, is a fundamental rethinking of our values and assumptions not only about justice, but about life in general. We need a new "lens"—a cultural and moral vision, if you will—that can span some of our differences.

Our interconnectedness

A new, life-giving lens calls for an approach that:

- favors compassion and collaboration above competition
- emphasizes responsibility as well as rights
- encourages respect and dignity instead of promoting shame and humiliation

- promotes empathy and discourages "othering"
- acknowledges the subtlety and power of trauma and the importance of trauma healing, and
- reminds us that we as human beings are not isolated individuals but are interconnected with one another.

Restorative Justice offers an example of a moral vision or compass that points in this direction. It also provides some practices that can help us live the vision.

Restorative Justice may or may not be "the" vision, but perhaps, at least, it can be a catalyst. It is, at minimum, a call to reexamine our assumptions, to take stock, to have a conversation. It may also be viewed as part of a larger effort to build a culture of peace, a peacebuilding approach to justice.

The concept of Restorative Justice has roots and resonance in many indigenous, cultural, and religious traditions. It connects with these, sometimes helps to legitimatize them, yet is not necessarily rooted in any one of them.

As a field of practice, Restorative Justice arose as an attempt to respond to crime but today has moved far beyond that to many

An example of RJ being applied to historical wrongs is told in the book, *Cousins: Connected through slavery, a Black woman and a White woman discover their past—and each other*, by Betty Kilby Baldwin & Phoebe Kilby. *The Baltimore Sun* called the book a "two-woman, racial reconciliation juggernaut."

other areas of application. It is increasingly popular in education settings. It is helping to reframe conflict resolution practices. It is also being applied to historical wrongs, such as the legacy of slavery in the U.S.

To review, Restorative Justice is essentially a needs-based, relational approach to justice issues. It focuses on repairing harm and promoting responsibility. And it favors dialogue and consensus as a process for doing so. RJ is a value-based orientation, centering values such as respect, responsibility, and relationships.

The goal of this vision

The overall goal of a Restorative Justice approach to all of life is to promote individual and relational wellness—to improve the health of individuals and communities.

Restorative Justice changes the questions, or the emphasis of the questions, we ask about harmful behavior. Instead of a preoccupation with what laws were broken, who did it, and what punishment the offender deserves, Restorative Justice asks questions like these:

1. Who has been harmed? (The harm may be to individuals, communities, and/or relationships.)

2. What are their needs?

3. Whose obligation is it to address those needs?

4. What has caused this to happen?

5. Who has been affected or has a stake in what has happened?

6. What is the process that can involve them in the resolution and prevent future harms?

Questions like this can be used to guide responses to harm, even when no Restorative Justice program may be easily available. Clearly, these principles and values urge every one of us toward adopting this as our overall approach to life.

Restorative Justice practices

A variety of Restorative Justice practices can help to demonstrate and implement these principles and values. For example, victim-offender dialogues, or family group conferences that originated in New Zealand, provide a safe space for dialogue about what happened and what should be done about it. These are being widely used, not only in conjunction with the legal system, but also in schools, families, and workplaces.

Circle processes, sometimes called peacemaking circles, may be the most powerful, universal, and value-based approach. These are widely applicable to many situations beyond those where direct harm is involved and seem to connect with many indigenous traditions. In fact, they entered the Restorative Justice field from the Aboriginal community in Canada. Kay Pranis, an advocate and trainer of circle processes, finds them to be a practical tool for building community and achieving positive social change. The mechanics of the circle are simple. Participants sit in a circle without a table. One or two people—often called circle keepers—facilitate the process. A talking piece is used to regulate speaking. It moves in one direction, and only the person holding the talking piece is authorized to speak (although they may pass if they want to). Thus, no one is interrupted, and everyone has a chance to speak if they wish. This slows the process down and prevents people from talking over each other.

Often an early round involves a discussion of the values that participants wish to bring to the circle. The emphasis is upon establishing relationships before moving to the work at hand.

The circle is structured to include all voices, to treat everyone with dignity, to build connections, and to honor each member

About a year after the Timothy McVeigh Oklahoma City bombing trial, Tammy Krause and I led a small circle that brought together some of the defense attorneys and some of the survivors who had testified for the government. It was a powerful process as the two "sides" experienced and came to better understand the other's perspectives.

as belonging to the whole. The circle slows us down and creates space for deep listening, allowing us to hear our own inner voices while hearing the voices of others. This in turn provides opportunities for empathy, reconnection, truth-telling, and healing.

Kay sees this as a way of building community and, beyond that, a form of radical, participatory democracy. The threat to modern society, she says, is not primarily the lack of math or science or technological skills; rather, it is the lack of skills and opportunities for living together and for building a culture of peace.

Restorative Justice, then, is not just about responding to crime or even harms. It is a way of approaching life.

An approach to all of life?

When people first suggested that Restorative Justice was really "a way of life," I thought, how could an approach designed to address the shortcomings of the criminal justice system be thought of so grandly? Eventually I realized that it is the values and principles, the overall vision, of Restorative Justice that can belong to all of life.

Legal systems are designed to say something about how we live together, but they only define *minimum* permissible behavior in a society. They usually draw these boundaries by threatening harm to those who cause harm.

Restorative Justice, on the other hand, provides a more comprehensive moral vision of how we should live together. The values we need are built into the concept. It is a vision that acknowledges our interrelationships and provides some values and principles for maintaining and repairing those relationships. (See the next chapter, "10 Ways to Live Restoratively.")

A compass more than a blueprint

Restorative Justice must not be considered a blueprint to be followed in detail. Practices, even the concepts, must always fit the setting. Even after more than multiple decades of living and applying Restorative Justice, many questions still exist.

Perhaps Restorative Justice is instead more of a compass, pointing a direction and providing an invitation to question and explore our values, our needs, our traditions, and our visions.

Many academics who research and write about Restorative Justice are social scientists. Science has an important role in this field, but so do the arts. Restorative Justice, like scientific innovation, involves a blend of science and art.

It is no accident that many of the innovators who were responsible for the development of computers and the internet were not only scientists but artists—musicians, painters, poets. Similarly, the early pioneers of Restorative Justice were drawing upon their creative instincts. It is such artistry that allows Restorative Justice to thrive and be adapted to varying personalities and settings. Although Restorative Justice needs science, I find it helpful to also view those of us who try to practice it as artists. My summary point is this: I suggest that we view our calls to service, our lives, our justice work, with the eyes of an artist.

Steven Meyers writes about the artist's perspective in his book, *On Seeing Nature*. He talks about the *art of seeing*, but it applies equally to the art of living and doing justice.

Meyers says ". . . one's knowledge must never overcome one's awe. As long as there is awe, there is seeing," and he adds, "Seeing is a process, partly, of replacing our arrogance with humility."

Or we can rephrase it: Living justly is a process, partly, of replacing our arrogance with humility.

"Seeing begins with respect," Meyers comments, "but wonder is the fuel which sustains vision."

Those two essential values!

I want to conclude by once again emphasizing those two values which have become very important to me.

The first is humility. We often think of humility as not putting ourselves forward, or not taking credit. But here I view humility as a deep recognition of the *limits* of what we "know." What we know, our "truths," are inevitably affected by who we are: our gender, our race and ethnicity, our experiences, our biographies. For this reason, we should be very cautious about generalizing our "truths" to other people and other situations. For this reason, we must be willing to listen to others and appreciate and be open to their realities.

Only by being and doing this can we live together in a restorative way. Empathetic or compassionate listening and respectful dialogue are essential.

The second value is wonder or awe. Western education and learning have been profoundly shaped by the philosopher Descartes. Descartes' methodology was one of skepticism: he was determined to doubt everything except what was truly undoubtable. As I've said many times, I had the good fortune of having a professor for one of my early philosophy classes who acknowledged this. He proclaimed that skepticism would not be our primary approach to the history of philosophy. Instead, he said, we would begin in wonder.

To quote David James Duncan in his book *My Story Told as Water*, "Wonder is unknowing, experienced as pleasure."

In Restorative Justice, we inevitably experience this kind of pleasure, if we are open to it. There is so much we do not know, so much to discover.

I will conclude with a story that for me illustrates this kind of wonder. It also suggests how Restorative Justice principles and questions might be used to shape interventions even in the absence of established Restorative Justice programs. We *can* choose to live this way.

In 1994, when Fred Van Liew was chief criminal prosecutor in Polk County, Iowa, he read a troubling police report. A local Jewish synagogue had been vandalized, with Neo-Nazi graffiti sprayed on it. An 18-year-old man and his 17-year-old girlfriend had been arrested and charged with the crime.

Fred says that he had been "irreparably damaged" by reading my early Restorative Justice book, *Changing Lenses.* As a result, he was unable to see things the way that he had been trained in the criminal justice system. He could have prosecuted these two people with a hate crime, but instead, he began to ask Restorative Justice questions.

Fred met with the leadership and some of the members of the synagogue, some of whom were Holocaust survivors. Many were angry, afraid, traumatized. When Fred suggested a circle process, many were skeptical. Eventually, however, they decided to proceed.

It was a difficult and moving process. Members of the synagogue were able to talk about how the vandalism had affected them. In turn, they heard the offenders' stories of hurt, loss, and alienation, and of finding a sense of belonging in a white supremacy group.

Eventually the members of the synagogue and these two young people came to an agreement. The offenders would do 200 hours of work for the synagogue; they would study Jewish and Holocaust history, led by synagogue members; they would finish their high school educations and find jobs.

They did all this, got married, and had a child. The rabbi and others were invited to the wedding and attended, bringing gifts. Five years later, the rabbi spoke at a conference about his friendship with these two, holding back tears.

This is an example of bringing a Restorative Justice framework to an uncharted situation. It was possible because of Fred's and the synagogue's willingness to be creative and take a chance. It is definitely a story that leaves me with a sense of awe and wonder.

In the Afterward to *Changing Lenses*, first released in 1990, I described Restorative Justice as *"an indistinct destination on a necessarily long and circuitous journey."* Now, more than three decades later, I can confidently say that, although it is still a journey with many curves, many detours and wrong turns, the road and its destination are not as indistinct as they once were.

I believe that if we embark on this journey with respect and humility, with an attitude of wonder, it can lead us toward the kind of world we want our children and grandchildren to inhabit.

●　●　●　●　●　●　●　●　●　●　●

I am often surprised by the testimonials I am offered about how RJ has affected—even transformed—lives. Several people, in fact, have told me that they changed career trajectories after reading my books. That's a scary responsibility!

Sometimes it is the philosophy of Restorative Justice— the "lens" that either reorients people or affirms their basic values. Sometimes it is the hope that RJ offers. Occasionally, for example, I have heard from judges and lawyers that it offers a hopeful alternative to their cynicism, re-energizing them for their work. I once received a postcard from a retired judge, now a ceramic artist, about one of my books. "This is an evil book," it read. What was evil, he went on, is that he was so engaged with the ideas that it was detracting from his pottery work.

. . . .

Sometimes it is what people have experienced through RJ processes.

At a conference a young woman came up to me and said, "I want you to know what RJ has meant for our family." They had been victims of serious crime, she said, which had especially affected her father. A victim-offender conference provided some healing for the family, however, and afterward her father decided to be trained as a volunteer facilitator for the program. Then one day in the city, her father ran into the person who had harmed them, and he immediately spoke about how that victim-offender conference had changed his own life.

"Now," the young woman said, "this is my life," explaining that she planned to go on for training to work in the field.

In an early RJ program, an older man participated in the training to become a volunteer victim-offender-dialogue facilitator but never facilitated any cases. One day the program received a call from his daughter. She said, I know Dad never facilitated any cases for you, but I want you to know how his experience affected our family. Our family was estranged; we didn't do Thanksgiving, we didn't do Christmas. After Dad took the training, he contacted all of us and said, We need to have a VORP (victim offender reconciliation process). We did—and we now have our holidays together.

. . . .

What difference might it make if we brought a Restorative Justice vision to the pressing issues of our day? To the systemic racism exposed by the killing of George Floyd and so many others, and by the Black Lives Matter movement, for example? To the wrongs committed against the indigenous people of North America and the world?

I used to begin my Restorative Justice course by asking participants to adopt a Zen Buddhist "beginner's mind"— that is, to have an attitude of openness, and to temporarily put aside preconceptions. How might we look at the issues differently if we did that? What creative responses might we imagine?

CHAPTER 13

Ten Ways to Live Restoratively

Over the years, sometimes in collaboration with colleagues, I have written a number of "signposts" as simple guides to applying restorative principles, for example, to working with those who have harmed or have been harmed. The 10 signposts below first appeared on my blog but have been adapted into a number of other forms since then.

Increasingly for me and many others, Restorative Justice is not just about crime or addressing wrong. It is a way of approaching life, and life together.

It's about taking our work home with us. It's why I'm energized by so many testimonies about how people have found ways to apply RJ in their daily lives.

When life-sentenced women at Muncy prison in Pennsylvania tell me they are keeping each other accountable with the question, "Is that the RJ way?," I realize that Restorative Justice is much more than a technique. It is about its values and principles.

Based on that, here are my suggested 10 Ways to Live Restoratively:

1. Take relationships seriously, envisioning yourself in an interconnected web of people, institutions, and the environment.

2. Try to be aware of the impact—potential as well as actual—of your actions on others and the environment.

3. When your actions negatively affect others, take responsibility by acknowledging and seeking to repair the harm—even when you could probably get away with avoiding or denying it.

4. Treat everyone respectfully, even those you don't expect to encounter again, even those you feel don't deserve it, even those who have harmed or offended you or others.

5. Involve those affected by a decision, as much as possible, in the decision-making process.

6. View the conflicts and harms in your life as opportunities.

7. Listen deeply and compassionately to others, seeking to understand even if you don't agree with them. (Think about who you want to *be* if you're having a disagreement, rather than just about being right.)

8. Engage in dialogue with others even when what's being said is difficult. Remain open to learning from them and the encounter.

9. Be cautious about imposing your "truths" and views on other people and situations.

10. Sensitively confront everyday injustices, including sexism, racism, and classism.

CHAPTER 14

Do We Need More Jails?

I am not sure that anyone has fully imagined what a restoratively-oriented justice system would look like. The New Zealand youth justice system, described briefly in the next chapter, does suggest some possibilities. However, in this essay for Mennonite World Review, *I suggested that addressing several fundamental problem areas is an important starting point.*

My community of Harrisonburg, Virginia, like many others, is facing a crisis of jail capacity. This is not a new issue. Many communities were wrestling with this in the 1970s and '80s when I first began working in criminal justice. Today, incarceration rates are much higher than they were then. The U.S. still leads the world.

I've learned two fundamental things over these years:

First, our systems are basically capacity-driven. We tend to fill whatever capacity is available. I remember research predicting that if you build a new jail, it will be filled in two to three years and will be above capacity in five. To quote from the movie *Field of Dreams*, "If you build it, they will come."

Second, simply providing alternative sanctions does not reduce jail and prison populations. Additional programs may be good to offer, but alone, they will not reduce incarceration. In fact, they may only expand the system's ability to take in people.

What is fundamental to the population of jails is the nature and structure of decision-making within the system. If we are serious about the issue, we must analyze the following:

1. Who makes the key decisions about arrests, charges, plea agreements, sentencing options? A starting point would be a flow chart identifying each of these decision points and the officials making the decisions in the justice system.

2. To what extent are these decision-makers *accountable* for their decisions, and to whom? Are they required to take system capacity into account in their decisions? What incentive do they have to do so?

3. What are the goals of their decision-making? What are the decision-makers, and we, trying to accomplish with these decisions? If our goal is primarily to remove lawbreakers from society and punish them, to make sure they get what they "deserve," then our jails and

prisons will be full, and victims' needs will continue to be sidelined.

A county in western New York illustrates what can happen when we address these issues. Faced with an incarceration crisis, the community adopted an imaginative approach that resulted in a reduced jail population. In the early 1980s, Genesee County, New York, faced a jail capacity crisis. While others were proposing a new jail, one candidate for sheriff, Doug Call, argued that the county did not need a new facility. He won and introduced programs including a process for determining outcomes that was victim-centered. The new process held offenders more directly accountable, and it was much more collaborative among all the stakeholders and decision-makers, including prosecution, defense, victims, and even offenders. Last I heard they had not built a new jail but were renting out space to neighboring counties.

My point is that no matter what our concept of justice, the only way forward is to create more clarity and transparency about our decision-making and more accountability for our decisions. Above all, our communities need more conversation about what we want to accomplish with justice and how we can best achieve those goals.

Perhaps the jail crisis can be an opportunity to explore these issues.

* * * * * * * * * * *

Although there are various points in the American criminal legal system where the three questions above are important, the prosecutor's office is of particular significance. A number of analysts have pointed out that prosecutors have tremendous power in our communities, and that because at the state and county level they are mostly elected, we in the U.S. have the most politically-oriented justice system in the Western world. This provides a significant challenge, but also perhaps an opportunity.

Former prosecutor Fred Van Liew's story in Chapter 12 is an example of what is possible, but it is also a warning. Prosecutions dropped significantly due to a variety of options when he was in office but when, he reports, the prosecutor who replaced him went back to the old ways, traditional prosecutions rose sharply. Real change cannot simply rely on individuals but must be systematized and rooted in the community.

The communities in various countries seeking to be "Restorative Cities" perhaps suggest one way forward. New Zealand's approach, described briefly in the next chapter, is another.

In Brazil, judges and prosecutors have been some of the leading proponents of community-oriented Restorative Justice. In this photo, my then-colleague Carl Stauffer and I are presenting to a group of judges from Nepal visiting our program for training.

CHAPTER 15

New Zealand's Unique Approach to Youth Offending

I have had the privilege of visiting and working in New Zealand many times and was asked by the magazine "New Zealand Inspired" to write something about my experiences. I chose to write about their inspiring youth justice system.

New Zealand's youth justice system, described briefly below, is far from perfect. But it does suggest possibilities about how a restorative approach and a modern legal system might be integrated. In fact, Impact Justice here in the U.S. has adapted its approach in some communities as a way of keeping young people out of the criminal legal system altogether.

Okay, I confess, I love New Zealand. If it weren't for my grandkids here in the U.S., I'd consider moving to Aeoteroa. The land is gorgeous, the people and culture hospitable, and you can get a decent short black espresso almost anywhere. But then there is the clincher: New Zealand has the only youth justice system in the Western world with a Restorative Justice core. I've had the opportunity to visit on a number of occasions, including as a Fulbright Senior Specialist with Auckland University of Technology's new Restorative Justice Centre—and I take any opportunity to return.

In the 1980s, New Zealand was faced with problems familiar to most Western countries: very high incarceration and foster care rates for young people, disproportionate numbers of minority youth in the system, and charges of institutional racism from the indigenous Maori community.

After listening to the voices of various communities, Parliament responded with the Children, Young Persons, and Their Families Act of 1989. Without really being aware of the Restorative Justice movement, they had created the first Western legal system that put Restorative Justice as the intervention of choice, with courts serving as a backup. Later contact with the Restorative Justice field helped them to fine-tune the system, for example, by putting more emphasis on victims' needs and roles.

The Act recognizes what most criminologists know: If we label youth as offenders, they are more likely to become such. Thus, it instructs police to release youth who commit less serious offenses with a caution or minor intervention.

Most serious crimes are expected to go to a family group conference (FGC) involving the youth and their parents, victims and their supporters, police, a youth advocate, and sometimes others. This group is charged with deciding, by consensus, the outcome of the case, including any necessary compensation for the victims.

The youth court handles cases in which responsibility is denied, or cases of murder or manslaughter, but it still may refer the case to an FGC once the case is adjudicated. It is a brilliant concept and, where practiced as intended, highly effective. It has, for example, drastically reduced rates of secure lockup.

But nothing in the real world is ever perfect. The system still has a number of glitches, and its implementation is uneven in various parts of the country. And although there have been some efforts to apply Restorative Justice to the adult system, its impact there is still fairly peripheral. Paradoxically, in fact, the country with such an inspired youth justice system also has [at the time this was written] one of the highest incarceration rates for adults in the world.

New Zealand's youth justice system is an important beacon for the rest of the world. "Don't mess it up," I told practitioners on my recent visit there. "If you do, you mess it up for all of us. The world is watching."

"That's a heavy responsibility," responded Principal Youth Judge Andrew Beecroft.

New Zealand had no map to guide them as they pioneered this work. Thanks to them, the rest of us do. We have some idea about what routes are successful but, also some of the hazards along the way. The responsibility, then, is not only theirs. We are watching, but hopefully we are also learning from them.

• • • • • • • • • • •

I appreciate unprompted testimonials. Once Judge Fred McElrea and I were being prepared for an interview on New Zealand TV. The woman doing our makeup asked why we were there. When we told her, she described how her brother had gotten in trouble and things had been resolved through a family group conference.

New Zealand did not know about Restorative Justice when this youth system was initiated. However, thanks especially to the Maori perspective, the new system included many restorative elements. When Judge McElrea, Chris Marshall, and others discovered Restorative Justice and introduced it to New Zealand, that perspective served to tweak the system, for example, to make victims more central.

New Zealand institutionalized their answers to the questions in the previous chapter by establishing the basic principles in law. Alan MacRae, a leading practitioner of family group conferences and co-author with me of The

Little Book of Family Group Conferencing, New- Zealand Style, *used to say that practitioners did not need a lot of rules and guidelines as long as they keep the basic principles in their pockets and refer to them often. From Alan I learned to appreciate "principled-practice"—practice grounded in principles rather than slavish obedience to rules, procedures, or specific practice models.*

Fishing with Alan MacRae (below),
South Island, New Zealand 2002

. . . .

I am something of an espresso geek. I roast my own beans and brew with an espresso machine that I have equipped with a micro-controller to precisely manage temperature. When we first were invited to New Zealand in 1994 it was a tea culture, but as we returned over the years it transformed into an elite coffee culture. A Ristretto is a very concentrated, rich espresso—quite rare in the U.S. This one, in a coffee shop near Wellington, was probably the best I've ever had.

. . . .

This reminds me of my first visit to Brazil in 2008. When I landed, the woman who picked me up at the airport asked what I wanted to do with any spare time, probably assuming I'd want to visit the beaches. I said I would like to know what Brazilian photographers were doing and that I was a coffee lover. She laughed: her mother was a well-known photographer and her family owned a coffee farm. She immediately took me to meet her mother, and I spent the last 24 hours of my visit on their coffee farm.

Astro Coffee Farm, Brazil

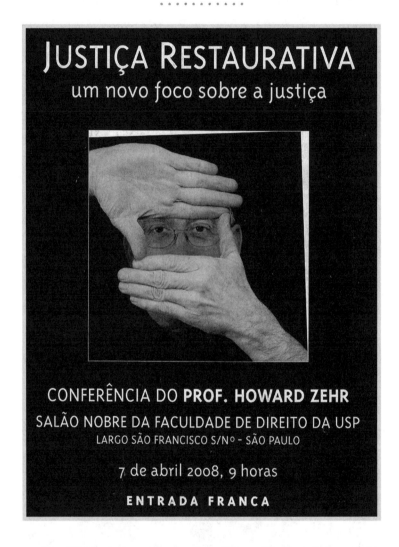

The 2008 visit was in conjunction with the release of the Portuguese edition of my book Changing Lenses, *published by Palas Athena. The above poster announced the events.*

On my last visit to Brazil, in 2015, one of my lecture venues was the grand hall at the law school in Sao Paulo. Happily, my Brazilian lawyer friend Luis Bravo made sure I had an excellent espresso on this trip as well.

CHAPTER 16

Education on the Healing Edge?

In August 1996, early in my teaching at Eastern Mennonite University, I was asked to address the faculty and was given the topic "On Becoming a Christian University of Distinction." EMU had just adapted "A Christian University of Distinction" as a tagline, and I was a bit uncertain what it meant or how I felt about it.

EMU, the home of what is now the Center for Justice and Peacebuilding, is a relatively small institution, founded in 1917, and connected to Mennonite Church USA. Although denominationally-based, the university has a strong commitment to global concerns and a diversity of faiths and perspectives, and this is especially true of CJP, where most of my teaching was. Throughout its 25-year-plus history, CJP's Summer Peacebuilding Institute has annually brought together practitioners and other learners from 40-50 countries and many faiths and traditions. Similarly, the residential M.A. program has been highly diverse.

As I try to make sense of the awkward phrase, "A Christian university of distinction," and what it means for education, my ruminations inevitably turn personal. I've come full circle, back to where I started my vocational life: in higher education. Twenty years ago last spring I left full-time teaching at Talladega College in Alabama to pursue practice and public education. Although my teaching experience had been a positive one, I never believed that coming back to teaching and university life would sound like good news. Today, I'm happy to report that it is!

The world has changed in those years: students are different, but I'm different as well. It is in this setting of experience and change that my comments emerge: what follows is what I have learned through educational environments in both public and academic arenas. I am going to talk about what we know, how we know, and what this implies for education.

As the first White graduate of Morehouse College, and later as a European-American teacher of African American students at Talladega College, I found myself immersed in a world different than the one I had known. I was forced to become aware of how fundamentally our values, our worldviews, our approaches to education, are shaped by culture and ethnicity. The influence of ethnicity and culture is far-reaching and subtle, beyond rational analysis, beyond consciousness, at the core of who we are. It's more basic than we know, even when we think we know.

As a result of these experiences, I'm convinced that our ways of knowing, teaching, and communicating are profoundly shaped by our biographies. What we think we know, how we come to know it, how we use what we know—all of this is molded by our gender, our ethnicity, our culture, our history, in ways that most of us, in spite of our best efforts, understand very incompletely.

Higher education in the West has been predominately individualistic and competitive. It has emphasized performance and assessment. It has depreciated the life experience, knowledge, and styles of learning that students bring to it.

Educational structures have assumed the authority of the instructor. They have emphasized the superiority of the rational, the analytical, the verbal. The Cartesian principle of doubt and skepticism is often the starting point, but in the end, academics are taught to project self-confidence.

Christian education in particular is often associated with dogmatic, hierarchical, imposed ways of knowing, and an assumption of certainty about what we know. Higher education has helped to feed what Deborah Tannen calls "... the argument culture," which rests on the assumption "... that opposition is the best way to get anything done."

As a result, ". . . we prize contentiousness and aggression more than cooperation and conciliation."

This traditional approach to knowing does not work for everyone. According to the study, *Women's Ways of Knowing*, it does not work for many women. It has not worked well for me.

What is missing from our Western approach to education, I think, can be summarized in these two attitudes, which I have highlighted before in other circumstances: humility and respect. These values are what I think of when I think of becoming a Christian university of distinction. This attitude implies a deeply-rooted humility about what we "know" and how we use what we "know." It assumes that we:

- Understand the limits of the validity and generalizability of our knowledge.
- Acknowledge the role of our biographies in shaping our knowledge.
- Develop an appreciation for ambiguity, paradox, and mystery.
- Become conscious of the unintended consequences of knowledge and of action.
- Affirm multiple ways of knowing and presenting what we know.

It means that as teachers we put less emphasis on being experts and imparters of knowledge and more on becoming "learning facilitators." It means a deep appreciation for differences in what people know and how they know.

Above all, becoming a Christian university of distinction means a profound respect for each, for those who are "other" as well as those who are "similar," for students as well as colleagues.

We experienced what this means in a Summer Peacebuilding Institute course a few years ago, which was subtitled, "Lessons from Indigenous Justice." Although I coordinated the course, the two primary instructors were Alan MacRae from New Zealand and Rosemary Rowlands from the Yukon. Rosemary, an Aboriginal woman who has worked with what has come to be called "sentencing circles" and "healing circles," introduced the teachings and methodology of the circle, and we used this approach throughout the course.

The physical manifestations of this approach are a circular pattern for seating and discussion, and the feather or "Indian microphone." Behind it, however, is a philosophy: the "teachings." These teachings emphasize humility and respect. The discussion always moves clockwise, one at a time—not back and forth, argument-style. Only the person holding the feather speaks, and the feather reminds us of our responsibility to speak from the heart, with integrity.

The feather and the circle also remind us that each person is there for a reason—each has something to contribute, each is to be respected, and all are equal. In the circle it is understood that all of us, including our leaders, are imperfect and are on their own healing paths.

Most participants talked about the course as a spiritual experience. Several, in fact, reflected at the end that it had been life-transforming for them. And this was a course in criminal justice! It was, I am convinced, the attitudes of respect and humility, communicated by the instructors and their approach, that made this holistic learning experience possible.

In a used bookstore in Athens, Ohio, earlier this week I consulted a "dictionary of difficult words and phrases." *Distinction*, it said, means a "conspicuous difference."

If we can build our institution on these two principles— respect and humility—we can be conspicuously different, a Christian university of distinction. Not on the cutting edge, but on the healing edge.

• • • • • • • • • • •

Thinking back over my two primary teaching careers— first at Talladega College, then at Eastern Mennonite University—I am struck by how much I have had to learn, and how much I learned from my "students." When I began teaching, my approach was modeled on what I had experienced in college and graduate school: lectures. Good lectures actually often worked for me as a student, but I soon learned their limits. One of my undergraduate professors reminded me from time to time that my learning style was not necessarily the norm. Today, in fact, I can't stay with a sermon that lasts more than 15 minutes!

At CJP especially, I learned to build on students' experience and knowledge—to be an elective learning facilitator—to, as one person has put it (and as I've noted before), create a setting where wisdom can come forth.

For a number of years Hal Saunders was on our board of reference at CJP. Hal had served five American Presidents, often as a negotiator. He participated in the Camp David Accords in 1978, for example, and helped to negotiate the Iran Hostage Crisis 1979-81. In later life, he launched The Sustained Dialogue Institute. I often think about what he used to say: the education that matters is education that helps participants to conceptualize their own experience.

. . . .

I've enjoyed offering portrait sessions to my students. A few years ago I found this portrait of Nikky Finney when she was in my photography class at Talladega College in the 1970s. Nikky is now a nationally-recognized poet, having won the 2011 National Book Award for Poetry. When I sent her this portrait, this was her reply:

"So it was YOU who took this photo. I could not remember. I have a tiny very battered copy.... I have always felt that this photo was the most revealing photo of me ever taken... especially because there is evidence in this photo of an early ink mark on my arm there beneath the bracelet. This was always an early sign to me that I would, for the rest of my life, be marked by and covered in ink. A true sign of my life's direction. I do not own a piece of clothing or set of sheets or purse or pocket in a coat that does not hold the blood of a pen. I was 19 in this photo. Maybe 18. You captured something no one has captured since. I am grateful to you."

I was sometimes asked to do photographs for CJP,
as in the photo above. Eventually I set up a portrait
studio in our office building and offered students
free portraits. As I phased out of active teaching, this
provided a way for me to learn to know some of them.

I was asked to photograph former student Leymah Gbowee
after she received the Nobel Peace Prize. Here she and I are
taking stock of the images to see if we have what we need.

. . . .

Thinking back... Imagining ahead

Sometime around 1990—give or take a few years—I
found myself sitting in the jump seat, behind the pilots, in
a C-130 Hercules cargo plane flying above the barren, war-
torn land of South Sudan, asking myself how I had come to
be there and what I was doing. This was my second photography assignment in South Sudan during the civil war. For

this one, I was based in the UN's Operation Lifeline Sudan Lokichogio camp in arid northern Kenya, catching relief flights in and out of Sudan.

It was a challenging assignment and for whatever reason—maybe because of the hardship and dangers, certainly because of the suffering I was seeing—I was tired and discouraged. Then an image came to me from a passage that had been assigned by my spiritual director before my trip.

Like the prophet Elijah, I was sitting under a desert tree, feeling sorry for myself, running scared. Unlike Elijah, I wasn't touched by an angel, nor did I receive a gift of food, but somehow that image and the implicit message—quit feeling sorry for yourself and get your rear in gear—helped me take stock and buoyed me up to finish the assignment. I often think of that image; it reminds me to affirm life and keep going.

I am frequently asked what has kept me going all these years, given the trauma I have listened to, the many obstacles encountered by Restorative Justice, the way that it has often been co-opted and misused. I think of what Julia Cass, former homicide reporter for the *Philadelphia Inquirer*, said when I asked her a similar question about what kept her going in spite of all the tragedy she had seen. "It's the strength and resilience of the family members and others I encounter," she said.

Similarly, for me, it's the testimonies of people whose lives have been changed by Restorative Justice, or who through great courage and resilience have transformed and grown from their trauma.

It is the surprising and inspiring ways those I have had the privilege to teach, mentor, and learn from have implemented Restorative Justice.

It is watching people grasp the ideas and go with them, often into new territory.

It is helping to make connections and observing the energy and creativity that comes from them.

I have, in fact, been in a privileged position in so many ways.

It is time for me to give up that privilege and, to the extent possible, bequeath it to others. I hope that this collection, limited though it is, can contribute to that transition.

I am happy to say that, although Restorative Justice is still a journey with many blind curves and possible wrong turns, the road and its destination are much clearer.

I end, as I did in the 25th anniversary edition of *Changing Lenses*, with this:

> *I believe that if we embark on this journey with respect and humility, and an attitude of wonder, Restorative Justice can lead us toward the kind of world we want our children and grandchildren to inhabit.*

To Howard Zehr

bikes: recumbent, foldup and upright

Morse code with a key
he's made of who knows what—
typewriter parts, dinner forks,
ten-penny nails for all I know

AM radios from sixty years ago—
the more that's wrong with them
the happier he is
and he'll fix yours
for fifty cents

espresso, from the beans
he roasts himself
adding milk would be a sin

Fuji XT-2's with researched lenses
panoramic photographs of trees and streams
images of pickup trucks
(and if you're tired of yours
he'll find someone to take your camera
off your hands
then make you think
you need another bigger better one
with the proper case, of course)

anything that's broke
he'll fix and make it better
than it was when it was new

emails you send:
if no reply
before the ink is dry
he's not around
or he is dead

and then there are the jokes
it's good his mother doesn't know

things most who think
they know this man
don't know about,
think all he does
is write his tomes
that show new ways
of bringing justice
to the world
(father figure of it all)
a man who goes to jails
and photographs and interviews
to show us who they are,
those people in the cells,
and who we are

but most a man
who when you talk to him
makes you feel
you're the only one
in the room
even in a crowded coffee shop,
that what you say is vital stuff
no one's ever thought about before.

—Joseph Gascho, photographer, poet, cardiologist, friend
2 July 2020

Acknowledgments

As I noted earlier, this book would not exist without the vision and encouragement—may I even say gentle prodding—of publishers Merle Good and Phyllis Pellman Good. Phyllis's careful selection, editing, and sense of the potential readership has been critical in shaping its final form. I am thankful to them for publishing not only this book but my earlier ones released under their previous Good Books imprint. I also appreciate Cliff Snyder's gifts in designing this book, as well as some of my previous ones.

I wish there were some way to acknowledge the many others who have contributed to my journey: former "students," colleagues, incarcerated men and women, survivors of violence, family and friends, scholars and practitioners... the potential list seems endless. As I have often said, I am really a synthetic thinker, so most of my ideas probably come from somewhere else. The older I get, the harder it is to remember where.

Finally, I want to acknowledge my wife Ruby Friesen Zehr, who has stuck with me for well over half a century. She will tell you that it hasn't always been a smooth ride. She will also tell you—rightly—that I wouldn't be the man I am without her. She has been an essential partner on this journey.

Text Credits

Chapter 1, "Restorative Justice—The Promise, the Challenge." A version of this interview first appeared in *The Magazine of the Alternative Dispute Resolution Center of the Judicial Power of Nuevo León.*

Chapter 2, "Journey to Belonging." A version of this chapter first appeared in *Restorative Justice: Theoretical Foundations* by Elmar G.M. Weitkamp and Hans-Jürgen Kerner, © 2002. Reproduced by permission of Taylor and Francis Group, LLC, a division of Informa plc.

Chapter 4, "The Promise and the Challenge of Restorative Justice for Victims" first appeared in Safer Society (UK), No. 32, Spring 2007.

Chapter 6, "How I Got Here—A Conversation with Bruna Pali" took place in November 2019 and was originally published at www.restorotopias.com

Chapter 7, "Restorative Justice and the Gandhian Tradition." A version of this chapter first appeared in the *International Journal on Responsibility*, Vol. 1, Issue 1.2 (May), 2018, 5-7.

Chapter 8, "Looking Back on My Career and the Field." Permission to include this chapter in the collection was granted by Tom Porter of *Journal of Law and Religion.*

Chapter 12, "Beyond Crime: A Vision to Guide and Sustain Us." A version of this chapter was presented at the International Conference "Restorative Approach and Social Innovation: From Theoretical Grounds to Sustainable Practices" (University of Padua and AREA Science Park, 7-8 November 2018). A version was originally published in *Verifiche* (XLVIII, no. 2, 2019, 1-15), and in partial form in a volume with the same name as the lecture, Giovanni Grandi and Simone Grigoletto, editors, Padova University Press, Padova 2019, 21-27.

Chapter 16, "Education on the Healing Edge?" Permission to include the email excerpts on page 198 granted by Nikky Finney.

Photography Credits

Photos by Howard Zehr on pages 51, 136, 141, 153, 194, 195, 205.

Also photos by Howard Zehr on pages 125, 160, 161, 162—excerpted from *Still Doing Life: 22 Lifers, 25 Years Later.* © by Howard Zehr and Barb Toews. Reprinted by permission of The New Press. www.thenewpress.com

Photos by other photographers on these pages: 101, Aaron Johnston; 108, collage by Joanna Yoder; both bottom portraits on 139, Dick Lehman; 144, 207, front cover, and back cover—right, Jon Styer; both on 193, Rita MacRae; 216, Seng Pan.

Photographers of all other photos are unknown.

About the Author

When doing portraits of students in my CJP studio, I sometimes changed places with them and let them photograph me. As I often told my photo classes, it is only fair that a photographer be willing to be on both sides of the lens. This portrait of me was done in 2009 by Seng Pan from Myanmar in one of these sessions.

Widely known as "the grandfather of Restorative Justice," Howard Zehr began as a practitioner and theorist in Restorative Justice in the late 1970s at the foundational stage of the field. He has lectured and consulted in many countries. A prolific writer and editor, speaker, educator, and photojournalist, Zehr has actively mentored other leaders in the field.

In 1996, Dr. Zehr joined the faculty of the Center for Justice and Peacebuilding at Eastern Mennonite University, Harrisonburg, Virginia. He continues to hold the position of Distinguished Professor of Restorative Justice and is involved in the field through the Zehr Institute of Restorative Justice at the Center for Justice & Peacebuilding, Eastern Mennonite University.

Prior to this, Zehr served as director of the Mennonite Central Committee U.S. Office on Crime and Justice. From 1970 to 1978 he taught at Talladega College, Talladega, Alabama.

Dr. Zehr received his Ph.D. from Rutgers University and his M.A. from the University of Chicago. His undergraduate degree is from Morehouse College in Atlanta, Georgia.

His many publications include *Changing Lenses* and the best-selling *Little Book of Restorative Justice*. Books involving photography include *Doing Life: Reflections of Men and Women Serving Life Sentences*; *Transcending: Reflections of Crime Victims*; *What Will Happen to Me?*; *Pickups: A Love Story*; and most recently, *Still Doing Life: 22 Lifers 25 Years Later* (with Barb Toews). In addition, he has exhibited his photography in a variety of venues, and his photos have been included in many publications.

Zehr is married to Ruby Friesen Zehr, originally from Manitoba, Canada, and has two daughters, Nicole and Kori, and two grandchildren.

This whole book is a container of hope, a must-have first-aid-kit to continue rescuing ourselves, and to continue guiding in the Movement of Restorative Justice.

One day after finishing his participation in a course about Restorative Justice in Oaxaca, I was the one taking Howard back to his hotel. I was excited about having my teacher with me to be able to ask him all the questions I had.

When I shot my first questions, Howard smiled and told me: "Let's talk about trucks."

He told me that to see old trucks still running was his enjoyment—to see them restored, tires, engines, batteries, little wires, and big headlights.

We arrived to the hotel and I felt very happy for having shared a moment with him. I thought he didn't want to talk about Restorative Justice anymore.

During his stay in the city, we continued sharing meals and drives; he was always kind and with his camera in his hands. Days later Howard sent me a picture by email. There, my daughter looks at me with her endless tenderness, and I get swept away in love for her.

It was then when I understood: Restorative Justice is everywhere, if we learn to put on the restorative lenses—the talks with our important people restore us, the wisdom of teachers (men and women) that teach with their heart; the old trucks that still run, the meals and the moments that make us see ourselves with different eyes, with eyes for the possibilities.

The picture of my daughter, taken by the person that has taught me the most about Restorative Justice and old trucks, is one of my favorite stories.

—Hector Valle, family therapist, circle keeper, Oaxaca, Mexico